MY FIGHT
WITH
GOD

MY FIGHT WITH GOD

He Won, and So Did I

BRIAN KLEMMER

DESTINY IMAGE® PUBLISHERS, INC.

P.O. Box 310, Shippensburg, PA 17257-0310

"Speaking to the Purposes of God for This Generation and for the Generations to Come."

This book and all other Destiny Image, Revival Press, MercyPlace, Fresh Bread, Destiny Image Fiction, and Treasure House books are available at Christian bookstores and distributors worldwide.

For a U.S. bookstore nearest you, call 1-800-722-6774.

For more information on foreign distributors, call 717-532-3040.

Reach us on the Internet: www.destinyimage.com.

Trade Paper ISBN 13: 978-0-7684-1041-9
Ebook ISBN 13: 978-0-7684-9116-6

For Worldwide Distribution, Printed in the U.S.A.
1 2 3 4 5 6 7 8 9 10 11 / 13 12 11 10

ACKNOWLEDGMENTS

God works through people and I have been blessed with many in my life. Certainly this book has been significantly enhanced through the careful editing by Julie, Jeff, Natalie, and Jennifer. Also to Tracy Shuman of Destiny Image Publishing house for managing the project. I would like to acknowledge Tom Willhite for showing me the Bible as the best "business" book, for opening me up to a personal relationship with Jesus Christ as both my Lord and Savior, and for the courage to withstand critics. To Ron Willhite, who is still a faithful minister in Roswell, Georgia, for simply staying the course. To Bob Harrison, "Dr. Increase," one of the most relevant ministers who has shown me not just his preaching but his personal life to be an example of what being a Christian is and for taking a chance on me as an unknown many years ago. To Pastor Aaron Lewis, for his creativity in various writing projects including this one. To Pastor Bill Livingston, (who has been the senior pastor at the church I attend) for simply putting up with me as well as challenging me to think. To John and Lisa Bevere, for their friendship, and the inspirational intensity with which they pursue Jesus Christ and the balance they are able to live out daily. To the many pastors that have honored me by allowing me to preach and disciple their people. To the many people who as paid team members or as a volunteers have stood up and spread the word about Klemmer & Associates literally around the world and allowed us to impact tens of thousands of people in a life-changing way. To my parents Ken and Alice Klemmer, for having faith in me that far exceeded what I had in myself. To my incredible wife Roma, without whose support I could not have done half of what I have been able to accomplish. And last but not least, to my three grown children Kelly, David, and Krystal, of whom I am very proud.

Endorsements

"The same vibrant, entertaining, and challenging style that characterizes and distinguishes Brian Klemmer as a trainer are found in the pages of this book, as he combines his own life stories with God's life-changing principles."

Ashley Schmeie
International President of Christian Outreach Centre Churches

"Real, real, real...fresh air. Brian Klemmer tells a story of spiritual life, not religious posturing. This is the biography for those who when they come to know God, will do real things for Him. The 'violent' life grabbers come to know the Kingdom. This book is for them."

Dennis Peacock
Founder and President, Strategic Christian Services;
author of *Doing Business God's Way*

CONTENTS

INTRODUCTION

Everybody seems to love a good fight, whether it's intellectual or physical. As a child, when you heard someone yell, "FIGHT!" you knew that everyone nearby would come running quickly to see who was involved in the big brawl. More than that, everybody waited around to see who was going to win. When I was a teenager, those kinds of quarrels seemed somewhat normal with guys brawling over a pretty girl or when someone mistakenly wound up on the enemy's forbidden turf. There is an excitement associated with seeing other people compete in such an animalistic manner, especially if there is no chance in being harmed ourselves.

What happens when you declare a fight with God? Who comes running to see that fight? I would think that many people would desire to see it—both to see the outcome and just to see who in the world could be that gutsy. Hence this book. It is quite obvious that anyone choosing to oppose GOD will be guaranteed a loss. Occasionally someone like Moses actually wins a fight with God (see Exod. 32:14) but for us we might wonder why we should even bother.

For me, I didn't know what else to do. And even if I didn't win, maybe I would at least be heard.

As a child I was raised Catholic. I went to Catholic school until the sixth grade at The Immaculate Heart of Mary in Baltimore, Maryland. My parents weren't deeply religious; the main reason I went to Catholic school was because at that time the school had a great reputation for giving a quality education, which my parents were strong advocates for. When we moved from Baltimore to New Jersey, I started going to public school. From that point on, I wasn't really exposed to a whole lot of spirituality, although I still attended church on Sundays all through high school. Later, when I went to West Point, I went to chapel services on the base out of a sense of obligation, but they really didn't have a major affect on me.

My view of church wasn't the greatest, nor was it a negative view. Really, I wasn't exposed to enough spiritual pathways to have a valid opinion one way or the other. My parents only went to church with me sporadically after grade school, mostly on holidays. I never remember reading the Bible or even owning one. God was out there somewhere; I just didn't have a clue where. When I did go to church, somebody would read the Bible and then someone else would preach, and boy, was it boring.

Don't get confused; it's not like I was an Atheist or Agnostic. I did want to believe in God because I had been taught that God is good, great, everywhere. But where was He for the soldiers suffering in Vietnam? Where was He for disadvantaged inner-city youth? Where was He for children starving just because they were born in the wrong country at the wrong time?

By the time I graduated from West Point in 1972, I was pretty mad at God and disillusioned. It seemed to make my whole spiritual voyage even more difficult. In the late 1960s, America was at the height of the Vietnam War. I saw so much pain and suffering in the world every time I watched television, listened to the radio, or read a newspaper. People were getting killed every day. Small children were being torn from their families and they didn't have food to eat or even adequate clothing or shelter. I thought, *Why would God just sit back and do absolutely nothing about the condition of the world that He supposedly created and loved?* It was pretty confusing to me. I, a mere mortal, would at least do *something*—so why didn't God?

My deal was that I would rather not believe in God if He could not help the dire situations or, even worse to me, if He just *would not* help. In many ways, that was the official announcement of my fight with God and a commencement of my journey of discovery that would last for the rest of my life. I can clearly remember when I was in the mess hall and they announced over the loudspeaker that one of our previous West Point cadets had been killed. After hearing that, I felt really unsettled inside.

From a soldier's point of view, I understand that there are times when war is necessary, especially when it comes to defending our country. So it wasn't a matter of right or wrong, moral or immoral—if you were sent into battle, you had to fight. In that social environment, I imagine that I first began to cultivate a mind-set about life in general.

> **My conclusion was, "Life's not fair!
> But it should be!"**

My conclusion was, "Life's not fair! But it should be!" Back then I was chasing mental rabbits, but now I realize that *fair* is a relative term. What's fair to one person is not necessarily fair to another person. Boy, I wish I had known that earlier. To live one's life continually pursuing the fairness of things amounts to a big waste of time, but I didn't know that then. Although I didn't think that God was fair, I still felt like I needed to know more about Him before I drew my final conclusions. God must have known my inner thoughts, as He was drawing me into Him.

I often pondered questions like, "What is the main point of life?" and so on. A friend of mine, Lance Giroux, went to a seminar that he claimed answered all of those kinds of questions. Not only was my friend getting answers to his questions, he always seemed to be happy. Drugs and racial tensions were major problems during that time, so how could he maintain such an upbeat attitude? What right did he have to be so happy? It made me very curious. Lance invited me to a seminar and told me that if I came with him I would better understand why he was always so happy. I wasn't really up to going to a seminar, but I asked him if there were any pretty women there. He gave me an affirmative response; and, being a single, 25-year-old man, that was enough for me. I was on my way.

A man named Bob Lipske conducted the first seminar that I went to. Tom Willhite, the founder of the seminars, conducted the next seminar. Although it was a public seminar, it was all about Kingdom principles and their practical application and the founder would often quote Scriptures from the Bible. One of the reasons Christianity hadn't appealed to me before this point was that most of the people who were Christians, at least the ones I saw, were broken and always got trampled on by the rest of the world. There was a stigma associated with them that I wanted no part of. Tom, however, was different in that he was a "man's man." He owned and flew planes, owned a 2,000-acre ranch, was married and had children; he ran a company and traveled the world. He appeared to do *what* he wanted, *when* he wanted, because he had control of life. He made the Bible real by showing me how it could help me at work, in my relationships, in my finances, to increase in business, and so forth. So it gave me hope.

Tom's grandfather, father, and brother were Pentecostal ministers and very strict ones at that. However, Tom was a totally different kind of guy in that he wasn't like your ordinary Christian at all. His brother was a Bible school scholar, a very learned man in the Scriptures. Tom, on the other hand, had gotten kicked out of Bible college. He was rebellious, which appealed to me.

I saw Tom make an incredible difference with not just businesspeople, teachers, housewives, and ordinary people, but I saw him do a project in Hawaii State prison and change many hardened criminals. I resigned my officer commission and went to work for Tom. Although I only knew him for another 6½ years until he died in a plane accident, he was my greatest mentor and I will owe him for eternity. He asked me if I wanted all the "things" he had, whether it was the marriage, freedom of time, the toys, or the lifestyle. Those were all of the things that I wanted to have in life, but did not know how to get. Like a kid in a candy factory, I said, "Yeah!"

He said, "If you really want all this, you will have to read the best business book I know."

I told him that that was not a problem because I loved to read. After promising to carefully read this "business book" that he claimed would provide all the secrets to a successful life, he then instructed me to buy and read a red-letter version of the King James Version Bible.

I was shocked. Never would I have thought that the Bible would be recommended reading for business and personal success in life. I thought that the book he was referring to would surely be a popular title picked from the business section. Although I had my doubts, I started reading the Bible and learning life's lessons from it. For the next six years until he died, Tom forced me to make the Bible relevant. He would often open a Bible during a business meeting and say, "How does this story or that verse pertain to what we are doing here?" I began to understand Kingdom principles, and later, I developed a personal relationship with Jesus Christ.

It was not a quick process for me. In my viewpoint, there are some Christians who know Jesus Christ as their personal Savior and are saved for eternity; yet they don't understand Kingdom principles, so their lives are consistently lacking and disappointing. Other people have what could be called "worldly success" with great marriages, jobs they like and that pay well, the ability to contribute to their society and make a difference, or even just a comfort with their self-identity. However, these people could still be lacking a true relationship with God. Kingdom principles, like giving, work for a nonbeliever just as much as they do for a believer in Jesus Christ.

Tom seemed to have everything, a successful life in relationships and business, plus a deep connection with God. Tom mentored me like a dad would his son. One of the earliest lessons that he taught me was to tithe. He did it to work on my scarcity thinking. From early on in my relationship with him, I began to tithe, or set aside 10 percent of my income to God. Although I was tithing, I still hadn't become a Christian and gotten saved at that point! Tom was only trying to teach me a Kingdom principle relating to giving and abundance.

I guess I was still waiting for the right time. I wanted to be able to tell the difference between what Christianity was and what it *wasn't*. So through my journey, the Bible became increasingly relevant to me as it began to address my day-to-day issues. The Bible helped me to become a better businessperson. That was a major drawing card for me. A lot of Christians get drawn to God because of guilt and remorse for the horrible things they have committed, but I didn't feel the need to be relieved of guilt. Quite honestly, I never thought of myself as a bad person. I saw evildoers as the ones who needed to get the guilt off their shoulders, not me.

Tom masterfully used the Bible to teach the principles of the Kingdom. He used the Bible to let me know that if you want worldly things, you can use the principles of the Kingdom to get them. Tom also used the Bible to inform me that if you want life to work effectively and successfully, you follow Kingdom principles. As I learned these principles, I learned about the King. Then I wanted a relationship with this King, and that's what made me want to become a Christian. Those are two distinct things—having a relationship with Jesus Christ as both Lord and Savior and knowing how to apply Kingdom principles. Both are important. As I continued to read the Bible, however, I would come across some really challenging texts of Scripture that didn't seem "right" or even make sense. They didn't seem fair. This started to get in the way of a personal relationship with the King.

Consider Job, who we are told in Job 1:1 *"was blameless and upright, and one who feared God."* That's a pretty righteous man. He loved God, loved his family, was an astute businessman, and worshiped God every day. In one day, however, Job's entire business was wiped out; all of his property burned down and all of his children were killed. The only family member left to help mourn his great loss was his wife, but she turns on him and begs him to curse God and to commit suicide.

To me, that story sounded a bit crazy. No, it sounded really crazy and grossly unfair. I certainly wouldn't do that to someone I loved. Why would God do that to Job?

As I began to read through the Bible, I discovered that Job wasn't the only guy who got the short end of the stick in life. There were quite a few others. And that is what this work is about. It's how I've dealt with some of the most difficult and unfair (from my point of view) texts in the Bible. The real thing is that in each of these "unfair" stories there is a great lesson, or shall I say, a greater and deeper message to be learned. It's really amazing how God will allow something that is seemingly unfair to become a saving grace when taken in its proper perspective.

If you are anything like me, these stories may make you mad, make you cry, and even make you question yourself or your faith. This book is written for anyone who is, or who ever has been, mad at God for any reason. Perhaps you have put your heart and soul into a relationship, only to have that person leave you—and you also feel like God left you as well. Perhaps you lost a loved one, or cried out to God to help you with the bills, and nothing seems to have happened. This book is for you. This book is also written for any Christian who has felt guilty for questioning God's wisdom. I have seen many a Bible study where people have questions but are so afraid of the judgment of their fellow Christians that they will not ask them. This book is also for you. This book is written for any thinking individual who has read the Bible and had problems with it.

My viewpoint is that God is OK with you disagreeing with Him. He's OK with you questioning His existence. Your very debates with Him can be the food that fuels a deep and loving relationship, no different than if you have had arguments with a spouse or child and it has deepened your respect and relationship. That's how it's been with me. So I encourage you to have your own arguments with God.

This book is not meant to be "the interpretation" of any particular Scripture. It is meant to let you know that it is OK to pursue with your own understanding the word of God as revealed in the Bible. If it assists you in understanding any Kingdom principles better and thus creating the fulfilling life you were meant to have, then I am excited. If it deepens your own personal relationship with Jesus Christ, then I am absolutely thrilled. The Kingdom principles of the Bible have supported me in tackling the challenges of my life. I went from being single and unable to create an intimate relationship to being happily married for 26 years with three great children as of the writing of this book. I went from having no career purpose to founding Klemmer & Associates Leadership Seminars, which did business in nine countries last year, impacting tens of thousands of individuals' lives in a significant way with our seminars. People attend the seminars to produce certain results whether it is losing weight, making a marriage better, discovering their purpose, or increasing their income. Through a series of exercises and games, they experientially explore their belief systems that are preventing them from achieving those goals (www.klemmer.com). Even a single practical application of James 2:17 has allowed me to raise millions of dollars for charity back when I didn't make much money, didn't know many wealthy people, and had never raised money previously. The principles have NOT given me a life without problems. Early in my career I was naïve and although I was making a lot of money I had no insurance. Someone saw that and I lost $500,000 through the legal system. I fought with God about the fairness and asked Him "why me?" What I heard from God was "why not me?" With God's grace and guidance following the Bible's principles, we made it all up and more in the following 18 months. What wrestling with God and the Scriptures has done for me is not only increase my closeness to Him but increased my ability to overcome the challenges that are a part of anyone's life. At the end of each chapter I will include some benefits I have enjoyed by wrestling with God and that particular piece of Scripture. They are meant to inspire you to look and see how you might benefit from wrestling with that Scripture or any other Scripture that has puzzled you, not as any form of boasting that what I have accomplished through God is in any way special.

Have fun arguing with God. As you digest the precious truths that God wants you to gain from it, you'll be bigger and better than you've ever dreamed before. And remember, if you fight with God and survive, you will surely be able to win every other fight in life. I did, and so can you! And if you lose a fight with God, you still win.

I fought with God to try and be in control of my own life. I lost that fight giving up control to Him. In doing that, I won by being fulfilled and accessing a power to win bigger battles.

CHAPTER ONE

FIGHTING WITH THE PRODIGAL SON: A MESSAGE IN FORGIVENESS

*T*hen He said: "A certain man had two sons. And the younger of them said to his father, 'Father, give me the portion of goods that falls to me.' So he divided to them his livelihood. And not many days after, the younger son gathered all together, journeyed to a far country, and there wasted his possessions with prodigal living. But when he had spent all, there arose a severe famine in that land, and he began to be in want. Then he went and joined himself to a citizen of that country, and he sent him into his fields to feed swine. And he would gladly have filled his stomach with the pods that the swine ate, and no one gave him anything.*

"But when he came to himself, he said, 'How many of my father's hired servants have bread enough and to spare, and I perish with hunger! I will arise and go to my father, and will say to him, 'Father, I have sinned against heaven and before you, and I am no longer worthy to be called your son. Make me like one of your hired servants.'

"And he arose and came to his father. But when he was still a great way off, his father saw him and had compassion, and ran and fell on his neck and kissed him. And the son said to him, 'Father, I have

19

sinned against heaven and in your sight, and am no longer worthy to be called your son.'

"But the father said to his servants, 'Bring out the best robe and put it on him, and put a ring on his hand and sandals on his feet. And bring the fatted calf here and kill it, and let us eat and be merry; for this my son was dead and is alive again; he was lost and is found.' And they began to be merry.

"Now his older son was in the field. And as he came and drew near to the house, he heard music and dancing. So he called one of the servants and asked what these things meant. And he said to him, 'Your brother has come, and because he has received him safe and sound, your father has killed the fatted calf.'

"But he was angry and would not go in. Therefore his father came out and pleaded with him. So he answered and said to his father, 'Lo, these many years I have been serving you; I never transgressed your commandment at any time; and yet you never gave me a young goat, that I might make merry with my friends. But as soon as this son of yours came, who has devoured your livelihood with harlots, you killed the fatted calf for him.'

"And he said to him, 'Son, you are always with me, and all that I have is yours. It was right that we should make merry and be glad, for your brother was dead and is alive again, and was lost and is found'" (Luke 15:11-32).

When I first read this parable, my response was, "You have got to be kidding me. This is messed up." It was more than unfair. What happened here was just not right and I couldn't understand why God had allowed it. Here you have a man, obviously very wealthy, with two sons. One is basically good, and the other is a screw-up. The screw-up comes home, and the dad throws a big party. What kind of a dad is that?! He rewards bad behavior with the one son and disrespects and antagonizes the good son. Why would I want to be like that dad? If it was me, I'd have just disowned the bad son. Cut him out. He made his bed; let him sleep in it. That's how I thought back then. What was

God trying to say…that good or bad didn't matter? That bad actually should be rewarded? That kind of God I didn't want any part of. Each time I reread the story I would get angrier and more questions would arise in my head.

My arguing with God around this Scripture taught me that I didn't get to decide what was fair, that I could have faith in big things and yet not live on a limb all the time, and that there are other things more important than justice, such as grace and mercy. Over the years that has assisted me in many ways, including bouncing back quickly from a bankruptcy and having bigger business success than before, as well as being more compassionate to my children and enjoying far better relationships than I would have enjoyed. But let us go back to the story and my initial arguments.

The younger of the two sons goes to his father and asks him for the part of his inheritance that he would receive upon his father's death. However, considering the fact that his father was alive at the time, it seemed to me that the son was disrespecting his dad with an insult. Even if a person is very old and sickly, it is tacky and insensitive to ask questions that suggest that they would be better off dead. That is the first thing that the younger son does that upset me. I imagined myself doing that to my dad and the pain it would have caused him. This younger son asks his father for money instead of celebrating the fact that his father is alive. When the son asks, his father does not give him any rebuttal at all. He simply grants him the request and divides up the portion that belonged to him.

The son took his money and squandered it in a far away country. Granted, it was his, and rightfully he could do anything that he chose to do with it, but my thing is that he did not do anything to reflect his parent's honor. What a person chooses to do with his or her money always carries consequences, sometimes good and sometimes bad. Not only that, what a person chooses to do with their money also reveals their truest character. From the looks of things, this younger son had a pretty bad character.

What's Not Right?

There are a couple of things that are just not right here. The first thing that didn't seem right is that no one should get something before the *right* time. There was nothing wrong with this young man getting money from his dad. But it seemed obvious that he got the money far too soon. He didn't earn it. And because of that, he really didn't know how to handle it.

When money is gained too soon, it is lost that much quicker. There are important lessons about money, which require a time investment, so that one can learn how to properly handle it. There is an old saying, "Quick gain, quick loss," and in my experience it's true. I have seen it a thousand times.

The old me was arrogant. (OK, I still am somewhat, but far less so.) I assumed that everyone thought like me; if by some stray chance they didn't, then they were wrong. Silly, I know, and it's embarrassing to admit it, but that's honestly how I thought. So either *I* was right, or *God* was right. I hadn't come yet to see how two different viewpoints could sometimes both be right. It's like when you have a mountain where one side is wet and the other side is dry. One person could say the mountain is wet, and another could say the mountain is dry. They are describing the same mountain differently, and yet both are right.

My one saving grace was that I respected Tom and his results, so I tentatively started to explore. What if the guy writing this story knew what he was doing and had a valid point? If he did, what message was he trying to communicate?

One of the things I now teach in my company is what I call "default drive training." Just like a computer has a default that it automatically goes to without any command, I suggest to all my employees that they should have, as their default, the idea that their supervisor or boss knows more than they do. Many have a hard time with this because they say this isn't true all the time. I tell them to always assume it's true anyway. If they approach their supervisor with, "I don't understand your thinking on this decision, would you mind sharing it with me?" then the 80 percent of the time they do know more, they will share it with you so that you can understand their reasoning. (He who knows *why* will always employ he who knows *how*.) In the 20 percent of the time that they don't know what you are seeing, this humble approach is more likely to cause them to shift their decision. It benefits you either way.

> ## He who knows *why* will always employ he who knows *how*.

With the character of the wayward son, was Jesus perhaps trying to communicate some lessons? I don't know. But I could get into that, and it gave me space to learn something instead of throwing the whole story out. Everyone knows that money is a means of exchange for goods and services. What the story seemed to show is that money is also a tool, a weapon that must be used properly; otherwise it can cause harm to you and others. No one in his or her right mind would give a child a gun and then send that child out unsupervised or untrained. Unknowingly, the child could easily cause injury to himself or others. The child may even mistakenly kill himself or someone else. He or she would not kill someone intentionally, but by mistake, because he or she was not properly taught how to use firearms.

With money, the rules are still the same. You have to be trained on how to properly handle money if you want to get the best use of it and not harm anyone. By obtaining it at a consistent steady pace, you learn the myriad of lessons around money: how to protect it, how to do due diligence, the different importance and impacts of cash flow versus net worth, how to get higher rates of return, risk versus reward ratios, and on and on. That's why a lot of sports players who get drafted to the pros fresh out of high school have a lot of potential challenges in life with regards to greed, promiscuity, self-indulgence, and chronic wastefulness. I'm not saying that all young professional athletes are the same with regard to their actions, or that all 18-year-old men are irresponsible. There is always an exception to the rule; you can always find a few very responsible young people who have their heads screwed on right.

Even in my own family, I have had to steel myself, because as a father you like to grant your child's wishes, but it often is ahead of its time. For example, one of my sons came to me asking for a $300,000 loan to buy a franchise, and part of me wanted to give it to him. The other part of me knew that because he was just out of college, had never had a long-term job before (let alone owned a company), that this was before his time. I turned him down, saying that although I could afford to lose the money, I could not afford to lose our relationship. If he lost the money, he may very well not know how to maintain his relationship with me nor I him. In the future, when he had more experience, it would be a whole different story.

In general, most young men cannot handle having $10 million, $20 million, and $30 million overnight, especially since many of them have not been trained to handle money, especially large sums. Giving someone who has had little exposure to massive amounts of money is a sure way of wrecking someone's life quickly. That's exactly what happened in the story of the prodigal son when this loving father gave his son his portion of the inheritance money. The son ended up going from riches to rags in a short amount of time.

In order to expand your wealth, you must have a measure of financial literacy and exercise financial responsibility. That is what causes people to succeed in the financial world and that is something that the prodigal son did not have. However, I realize that every man and woman must face his or her journey in life. Every person has to travel his or her path—including the father in this story. It may well be that the father knew that his son would not learn the needed lessons at home and that his going away with the inheritance was the best path for his son to take so that he could learn.

Man, that would take some serious caring about your son, wouldn't it? That would take some serious confidence in your son that he would turn out all right in the end. And this was the path that the father and the prodigal son chose to take. But despite all of that, I still thought that it was wrong for the son to ask, and for his father to give him that kind of money without first giving him a preparatory course on how to handle it.

FOOLISH PEOPLE SPEND *ALL* THEY HAVE

Of what use is money in the hand of a fool, since he has no desire to get wisdom? (Proverbs 17:16 NIV)

The next thing I didn't agree with was the fact that this guy went away to a far country and spent every single dime of his money. That's pretty foolish! But it all goes to show that money in the hand of a fool will always lead to futility. It would have been one thing if he only had about 10 percent left from what his father gave him, but he didn't have *anything*. Zero. Nada. My problem with this is that only a complete fool spends everything. Any rational, thinking person knows that you don't give away everything that you have. There are exceptions, like when you hear from God to do so, but as a general rule it is wrong because then you have no seed for the future. (Unfortunately, I know quite a few pastors who are incredible givers, except they do not give to their own investments and thus have to live less than God intended.)

You have to have something stashed away for a rainy day, or even a sunny day for that matter. It's just not right to spend everything, especially when you spend it on wasteful things that don't appreciate in value. The narrow-minded person spends everything, because they only think about today and not the future. I have seen a lot of people in the faith movement live this way. They are very sincere believers but become so faith-driven that they don't put anything away for the future or for business right now. In fact, this seemed to be a conflict with faith for me. That is because of "either/or thinking." Either/or thinking says that it must be one or the other but cannot be both.

I believe you can trust in God as a faith person and put away for retirement or to grow a church. This became very clear to me when I took a group of our Klemmer & Associates seminar graduates, who we call Compassion Samurai, to Uganda. Compassionate Samurai are bold ethical leaders committed to a world that works for everyone with no one left out. (*Compassionate Samurai* is also the title of my fourth book, which was a best seller in 2008). They each gave $10,000 to the people of Uganda through orphanages and building a purified water pipeline. In one orphanage where we gave the pastor a portion of the money, he said, "We are so thankful because it is hard to keep teachers when we don't pay them for three and four months." I was shocked until I saw the situation he was in. He had done incredible things with his orphanage and had trusted God to provide. To him, it seemed a lack of trust in God if he put money in a reserve—although it is standard good business practice. This caused him to be unable to pay his staff and to constantly live hand to mouth, among other problems. There is nothing wrong with keeping faith in big things and miracles but also making sure you have something to fall back on.

You never know when a famine may come in the land. When that happens, the foolish spenders will always have to beg for bread since they were not good stewards with the money they had during good times. Today and back then, it seems as if society somehow celebrates wastefulness. I'm not talking about lavish abundance here; I am simply talking about wasting what you have. There is a major difference between abundance and just being wasteful.

Abundance is really a great thing, while wastefulness is negative. Abundance means that you have more than enough, and because of that, you can share with others the overflow of your supply. With abundance there is no wasting at all; you simply give more to others from your reserves. So it is absolutely fine to celebrate abundance—something society needs to do.

In contrast, wastefulness is a serious problem. This can be seen in everything: how people waste food, time, natural resources such as water and natural gas, good opportunities in life, and so on. Nearly all people who mismanage money do so because they are wasters. If you write a bad check, you've just wasted money because you have to pay for the bad check fee associated with your mismanagement. That's wasteful. If you move from one house to another one every four or five years or even less, you are wasting enormous amounts of money since you are not creating equity in your home.

Many people buy into being wasteful by accident, because they falsely believe all the extravagances and flashiness accompanying wealth are worth it. In actuality, they are being wasteful while appearing to be abundant. People who choose that road are only mirroring the habits of the poor and in time will also become one of them. The prodigal son wasted all of the money that he had, which further proves that he should have never been given the money in the first place.

The Big Homecoming Celebration

Initially my disappointment in the father for throwing a party for the bad son blinded me to any lessons. When the prodigal son returned home and his father saw him far in the distance, the father became so excited that he started running toward his son to meet him halfway. He hugged him and kissed him. His son made a speech about how he was sorry for the bad deeds that he had committed and, if his father allowed, he wouldn't mind being a servant in his father's house. His father obviously thought that was a ridiculous request for his son to become a servant, since that was his own flesh and blood. Instead, he threw him a party and gave him expensive clothes to put on.

Every father in the world needs to celebrate his children, show them love, and create an atmosphere to help foster a positive and productive attitude about life. What made me mad was that the good guy, the faithful son, had never left home or did anything wrong and yet still didn't get anything. The son who stayed at home never embarrassed his father's name, never lived a wasteful and riotous life, nor did he operate with an impatient spirit. In fact, he showed more love for his father by not even considering his inheritance money prematurely. He just wanted to serve his father and be in his presence. But he was not rewarded.

The wasteful, rebellious, out-of-control and showy son who abruptly left his father's home before he was properly trained and mentored actually got rewarded for his bad behavior. Even if that is not so, it really seemed that way to me. The guy who does everything right doesn't get anything. That didn't seem fair. A lot of my struggle was centered on fairness, and it just didn't seem right that someone would have a party thrown in their honor for being wasteful. My thoughts were always that if somebody does good, reward them; if somebody does bad, punish them. What I came to realize is that God does not think that way.

What I Learned

While at first it was hard for me to accept this text, I had to review the whole story and look at it from the way that God may have seen it. While I was screaming, "Justice, justice, justice!," what I failed to realize is that justice cannot always be interpreted the way we want to see it. God, not man, determines what is just. Humans do not always know why things are the way they are, but God knows. Have you ever heard people say, "God knows best"? Well, I've come to discover that even if it weren't true, it's the most productive attitude to have! It is default drive training. During the times we cannot comprehend God's viewpoint, it doesn't change the facts, but it opens the door to revelation.

God, not man, determines what is just.

When you climb a mountain, the higher you get, the more you can see. If I am at the bottom of the mountain, I can only see from that viewpoint. God has a larger, higher viewpoint than I do. So I will only begin to understand God's justice when I am elevated to where He is. As long as I am on this earth, and as long as I think in terms of earthly things, I will not understand justice from His point of view. I'll have to climb higher up the mountain to understand the way God does.

Another thing that I had to accept is that mercy triumphs over justice. In my military mind, I kept forcing this text to be just. That's how I've always been wired. It was either black or white; there was no gray area for me, no compromise at all. But I discovered that deep in the heart of God is His merciful spirit, without which many of us would have been destroyed a long time ago.

Quite honestly, I've never been a guy who broke the law. To the best of my ability, I always tried to play life fair and square, never trying to hurt anybody. But even with my good intentions, I still fell short of being the total man that

God expected me to be. I found out that good intentions weren't good enough. And in those times when I fell short, God never threw me away. Instead, He showed me mercy. So if God was kind enough to extend His mercy toward me, then why should I try to prevent God from showing other people mercy, even if I don't think they deserve it?

It's pretty wonderful that we don't get what we deserve in life, but instead, we get His love.

I learned that we don't necessarily receive what we deserve when it comes to God. We receive what God is gracious enough to give to us freely, and that always exceeds what we actually deserve. This is really great news! It's pretty wonderful that we don't get what we deserve in life, but instead, we get His love.

I struggled with this story because, at one point, I really didn't think that the wasteful son deserved to be forgiven, or given anything in life, after his big mistake. If he wanted to be redeemed from his major blunder, he needed to earn his forgiveness. But then it dawned on me that, with God, a person doesn't have to earn forgiveness at all. You just get it. It almost seems like a "too good to be true" deal.

This story really wasn't about a prodigal son, his wealthy father, his staffed servants, or his "obey all the rules" brother. This story was really about me. It was about how I looked at life. It was a story helping me to discover what true forgiveness is and giving me a chance to put it into practice. In many ways, I hadn't forgiven God. When I would watch the Christian Children's Fund on television and see 40,000 kids starving to death or see the death and horror as a result of war on the news, it just didn't sit right with me. And what exactly was forgiveness?

Years after I became a Christian and started my own company, I was betrayed by someone whom I had considered a friend and who was also a senior person in my firm. I had trained him in the business, given him a part of the profits, and at one point he tried to steal our biggest client and go into business for himself. God gave me wisdom and protected our company in a strategy that prevented him from stealing our client. Then this individual wanted his old job back. I struggled as to what forgiveness was and whether or not I should take him back. My wife and some employees thought I was crazy for even considering it, but I was struggling with what forgiveness was. In the end, I decided I could forgive the person while still not entrusting them with certain responsibilities. It was much like a bank forgiving a loan but not making another loan until a track record is reestablished.

How many times have I let my anger at something I thought was unfair blind me to all the opportunities in front of me, robbing me of the gratefulness for what I did have? Enough to embarrass me, I am afraid. After my mentor died, his wife took over the running of that company. Many things changed. My wife kept encouraging me to start my own company, but I was afraid. Finally, after a Jonah-like experience, I decided it was time to leave. At that time, a close friend owed me $17,000 for flights and work done.

For a couple years I tried to recover that money, and then finally thought of the prodigal son story. I wrote a letter and forgave the debt—not out of nobility and being a moral Christian, but because I saw that the concern over this debt was blinding my creativity and energy that I could better use elsewhere. The truth was that I could make that money back in a good weekend—and I did, once I forgave.

The story of the prodigal son has been a useful tool for me in getting better at forgiving. My forgiveness always seems so small compared to what this father forgave. And it seems even smaller compared to the Father's forgiveness toward the people who killed His Son or even Adam and Eve who also betrayed Him.

Being a dad, I learned and am still learning through my children that regardless of the choices they make, I still love them unconditionally. I came to discover that part of forgiveness is mercy. It became clear to me that I really needed to work on showing mercy. Even if I showed mercy to some, I knew that I could definitely show more mercy to others if I made up my mind to do that, especially in the little things. At one point I realized I was working hard on forgiveness with the big experiences in life, but had been overlooking the everyday ones in my marriage and with my kids and employees.

I asked my Aunt Mary, the proud wife in a great 65-year marriage, what made a successful marriage. She responded, "Forgetting."

I blinked and said, "What are you talking about?"

She said, "Every time Uncle John does something I don't like, I force myself to forget within five minutes so that I go back to loving him the way I did before the event."

Incredible insight! I am not saying that forgetting is forgiveness, but it just might help in some cases to get you there.

Another thing I totally missed was that this son, despite all of the bad things he did, came back to his father's house with a true heart of repentance. He was willing to work as a servant. He did not ask for special favors as part of the family. Repentance is always a good thing. He came back not wanting to be served but rather to serve. It was an attitude of humility that made this man so well received by his father.

God doesn't measure your life by the negative things that you've done. He's really not keeping score at all. That's an incredible concept! If you're married, think about whether you keep score for both good and bad. You do, don't you? What about at work? Sad to say, keeping score is something that humans do a lot of the time. God is always waiting to receive you with open arms because He doesn't keep score. Repentance only helps to speed up the process, so that you can hurry up and get to the big party that He planned in your honor.

> **God doesn't measure your life by the negative things that you've done.**

In our society, a person pays for every crime committed against the law if he or she is caught. I thought that is how things worked in God's mind.

In some ways it is. The major difference is that when you repent, when you change your mind and your direction, you no longer have to pay for your mistakes or the things you did wrong. You'll discover that Jesus Christ paid the high price for all of our sins, in full. Changing your mind often equates to a change in God's mind too.

LESSONS FROM A PIG

So what else might God have been trying to communicate in the story? We can see here that the son has found himself penniless and instead of going home and apologizing right then and there, he decides to become a citizen of that country and find himself a job. He lands a job working on a pig farm, cleaning the pigpens and feeding the pigs. Having plenty of time to think, he begins to think about how stupid he had been, leaving his father's house and exchanging royalty for welfare. He's sitting with the pigs in a nasty, stinking, filthy pig's pen.

In my imaginative mind I see this pig looking at him, and the prodigal son staring back into the pig's eyes. No doubt, the pig was probably pretty confused as to why this young man would want to come and hang out with him. The pig knew that this man was a human, of far greater worth than a pig. Unfortunately, the prodigal son seemingly forgot his identity. You see, a pig will always be a pig. You can clean a pig up, put sweet-smelling perfume on it, and clothe him with royal garments. But at the end of the day, a pig is still a pig. The same dolled-up, freshly-bathed, sweetly-perfumed pig will go running headlong at the first sight of mud and filth. Why is that?

It is because you cannot wash away the mentality of a pig by dealing with their external appearance. The same concept goes for people. You cannot change a person by dressing them up and making them have the appearance of wealth and honor. It does not matter what they look like, but it does matter what is in their heart. What I mean by "heart" is that it matters most what is in a person's subconscious mind. The subconscious mind is the part of your mind that continually makes choices on autopilot, because it has been programmed over many years.

In order for a person to become wealthy they have to change their thoughts concerning wealth. For a person to become honorable they will have to adopt lifestyle traits of honor. One lesson that this pig can help a person to understand is that inner character matters very much, for you and for others. Another lesson is that no one changes in life until they choose to. No matter how hard you try to change any man or woman, they will not change until they know that change is necessary.

...no one changes in life until they choose to.

People do not change because you believe they should, but when they feel that it's necessary—something I will refer to as wearing sunglasses. Maybe you didn't know this, but pigs wear sunglasses too. When I speak of sunglasses, I don't mean literal sunglasses, although I love to use actual sunglasses to illustrate my point. The "sunglasses" I'm referring to are viewpoints or belief systems that people have. Those beliefs never change until one first becomes aware of them and then chooses to change them. Most people generally have belief systems about who they are based on what they've garnered from their environments.

One of the differences between a pig (or any animal) and people is the power of "choice." People have choices and animals don't. People have beliefs or viewpoints much like a pair of sunglasses. We have beliefs or viewpoints on risk-taking or playing it safe. We have beliefs or viewpoints on being self-centered or service-centered. People can choose to change their sunglasses or viewpoints. The prodigal son had a viewpoint of "entitlement" around his inheritance and he changed this viewpoint. The prodigal son had a viewpoint about what was important that radically changed.

What you believe about yourself and how you think in your subconscious is what you get in life. If you have always been exposed to limiting situations and believe that's the way it must be, then you will be limited in life. If you are exposed to unlimited thinking, but don't believe it, that is what you get.

Sitting amid the putrid smell of rotten food and decaying flesh, the prodigal son began to ponder, "In my father's house, even the hired servants live higher than I'm living right now. Why am I here? What am I doing with my life? I've got to go back home." He began to understand that he was not accustomed to this kind of lifestyle. It was foreign to his experience. But, for a moment in time, he had condescended and lowered his standard of life, not knowing that he had better options than the one that he was choosing.

Many believers are in the same condition as this prodigal son; they really don't get who they are. Due to experiences like a failed marriage, constantly working a low-paying job they don't like, being overweight, or being unsuccessful, they have created a false image of who they really are. Have you really embraced the reality of who you are? Do you really know that you are a king's kid? If you did, how would you be acting? Or has the exposure to negative things in life made you believe that you were anything less than royalty?

> **Once your thinking changes, your world will change too, as it did for the prodigal son.**

How we are raised, where we came from, or what "happened" to us may impact us in positive or negative ways. That is our choice (read the chapter "Facts Don't Mean Anything" in my book *When Good Intentions Run Smack Into Reality*). How we are raised or events that happen to us are like wind blowing in a certain direction. If you do nothing, you will be blown in that direction. However, you have choices available. You can move the rudder or a sail and go in the opposite direction. It overrides the wind or circumstance and choice can make it irrelevant. Look at the prodigal son. His upbringing was obliterated by choice. His bad choices on spending the money foolishly were obliterated by a new choice. What matters is that you belong to a royal family. Once you choose to recognize that, you will find that your thinking will change. Once your thinking changes, your world will change too, as it did for the prodigal son.

You can look at how some people choose to live and learn a lot from them. If a person wants to live like a pig, then that's fine for them. Just know that in life, you always have choices. This man realized that he had choice in the matter. Nobody was forcing him to stay in that situation. It was rather obvious that he was tired of being in the position that he was in, so he decided to go back home. Sometimes the lessons that you learn may come from the strangest places. The truth is that you are always being taught, whether you realize it or not. And whether you learn something or not is an entirely different story. Just know that life is not deficient of powerful lessons.

A Short Recap

• Justice is not interpreted from your point of view.

• You may not always know or have full understanding, but God does.

• God always determines what is just from unjust.

• Mercy triumphs over justice.

• God is a God of mercy.

• We don't get what we deserve; we get what God desires for us.

• Forgiveness is mercy.

• An attitude of humility will always usher in the Father's blessings.

• God never measures your life by the wrong things you may have done.

• Repentance speeds up your process, bringing you closer to the big celebration of mercy.

• Jesus Christ paid the price for you.

POINTS TO PONDER

1. Think back to the first time you read the story of the prodigal son in Luke 15:11-32. Did you struggle with the seeming injustice of it?

_____

_____

_____

2. When you read that story now, do you find yourself relating more to the prodigal son, the father, or the dutiful son? In what way?

_____

_____

_____

3. Have you ever felt like you got the short end of the stick? Have you ever felt that God allowed something negative into your life that you didn't deserve (illness, betrayal, loss, etc.) or that He failed to reward you for following His commands?

_____

_____

_____

4. Before moving on to the next chapter, spend some time in prayer. Ask God to help you weed out any feelings of resentment or anger from injustice, and trust Him to show you the fullness of His forgiveness, mercy, and grace.

_____

_____

_____

CHAPTER TWO

A RICH MAN CAN'T GET ENTRY INTO HEAVEN

*N*ow behold, one came and said to Him, "Good Teacher, what good thing shall I do that I may have eternal life?"

So He said to him, "Why do you call Me good? No one is good but One, that is, God. But if you want to enter into life, keep the commandments."

He said to Him, "Which ones?"

Jesus said, "'You shall not murder,' 'You shall not commit adultery,' 'You shall not steal,' 'You shall not bear false witness,' 'Honor your father and your mother,' and, 'You shall love your neighbor as yourself.'"

The young man said to Him, "All these things I have kept from my youth. What do I still lack?"

Jesus said to him, "If you want to be perfect, go, sell what you have and give to the poor, and you will have treasure in heaven; and come, follow Me."

But when the young man heard that saying, he went away sorrowful, for he had great possessions.

Then Jesus said to His disciples, "Assuredly, I say to you that it is hard for a rich man to enter the kingdom of heaven. And again I say to you, it is easier for a camel to go through the eye of a needle than for a rich man to enter the kingdom of God."

When His disciples heard it, they were greatly astonished, saying, "Who then can be saved?"

But Jesus looked at them and said to them, "With men this is impossible, but with God all things are possible" (Matthew 19:16-26).

Now this passage flat-out twisted my head around. It sure sounded like God wanted me to give everything away, and that being rich wasn't good because it would be even harder to get into Heaven. Let me tell you, this did not exactly excite me about Christianity. And then as I reread the passage, it got worse because then He said no one was good, so what was the point of trying?

Wrestling with this piece of Scripture taught me to focus on my relationship with God; that wealth was not only OK, but great as long as I had it in perspective; and that I had to work on my trust in God if I was going to relinquish the tight fist I had on control. Among the innumerable ways this has been of benefit is that with God I have been able to bless others with millions of dollars and I have not felt alone in making weighty decisions in running the business of Klemmer & Associates or raising our family.

Now the good thing about a passage or story that irritates you or gets under your skin is that it's like getting a little bit of grit in your teeth that you just can't seem to get rid of. You keep pushing at it and twirling it around. As I have said before, in this book, it is the continual wrestling match with God over pieces of Scripture that actually makes the Scripture meaningful and gives it value, as well as develops your personal relationship with Jesus.

Let's rewind to the beginning of this piece of Scripture where the young and rich ruler asks Jesus, "What must I do to have eternal life?" I gave the guy a point for asking a decent question. A lot of very financially wealthy people think that accumulating wealth is the end game. However, I had a gnawing somewhere inside me that told me there had to be more to life than having fun and accumulating material things. Unfortunately today, if you ask most teenagers, "What is success?" they respond with something around acquisition, consumption, or accumulation. Somehow I knew that wasn't it.

In the above Scripture passage, the rich young ruler is looking for eternal life or getting to Heaven. He is looking ahead—which is a good business practice, by the way. He may have asked himself the questions, "What happens after I die? What will happen after I am gone? Where will I live and with whom will I spend eternity?" Being a man who understood the value of making preparations, he asked Jesus questions about the afterlife.

For the most part, all world religions believe and tend to point toward an afterlife experience commonly known as Heaven. Christians believe and teach that Jesus Christ is the way to the truth and the life, and accepting Him as Lord and Savior is the way to get into Heaven. That is a very interesting notion because most religions teach about doing good things or being good and earning your way in. Even the rich young ruler is looking for instructions on how to get into Heaven: "Which rules must I follow?"

Jesus just flat gets him with a right cross to the jaw. "Why call Me good? No one is good."

Let me tell you, the rich young ruler (and me) was dazed and disoriented on the ropes of the ring.

No One Is Good

What I came to realize is that the rich young ruler misses it! I wish I could tell you I never missed the lessons my mentor gave me, but I would be lying. There were plenty of times my mentor was so blunt that it was like hitting me with a baseball bat, and I still didn't get it. That's the young ruler. Come on, if just anybody made the flippant statement, "No one is good," it probably would not mean very much. You wouldn't think twice about it. But when Jesus says, "No one is good," it takes on a very different meaning. Jesus never says words that are meaningless. Jesus was the most perfect one walking the planet. Even other religions take Jesus as a great prophet. At first reading this seemed to be saying Jesus himself was no good. If He doesn't have it all together, what chance have I got or did the ruler have? If no one is good, why try? On further study, it seemed Jesus was saying if He is good it's because of God and the goodness of God. Jesus is challenging the ruler not to look at the ruler's own goodness but to look to God. Every religion other than Christianity that I am aware of talks about living a perfect life and "earning" one's way to a version of Heaven. Jesus, instead of giving the young ruler an impossible standard of good things to do, is telling the young ruler to focus on his relationship with *THE* one who is good—God. Jesus might have said, "Nice counterpunch. That won't get you what you are asking for."

> **Jesus never says words that are meaningless.**

Still, the ruler misses it just as I did when I read it the first few times. The ruler persists in looking for the ultimate good thing he must do to get to Heaven because he is lost in that paradigm, and Jesus busts him again. Here you have a man, coming to Jesus, who is rich and clearly the leader of many people. It didn't even take this man an entire lifetime of investing to score big in the financial arena. This man is very young, and yet he is leading his generation with his personal business success. He's sharp, and yet he misses it!

You know, in a strange way, that gave me hope. Maybe I didn't have to be the brightest guy on the planet to get this Christian thing. In fact, I believe God is not a bigot. He would not just say that smart people, for example, are the only ones who get to Heaven. That would count too many of us out before we started.

Understanding proper protocol and knowing how to show respect for spiritual leaders, the young ruler addresses Jesus not only as "teacher," a name commonly conferred upon the rabbis of that day, but also added the word "good" before teacher to distinguish how much Jesus stood out from His contemporaries. He wasn't merely a teacher in the eyes of this fine young ruler, but an exceptional one at that. However, when this man refers to Jesus as good, he gets the surprise of his life as Jesus forthrightly rejects the compliment.

In a few short words Jesus devastated this man's ideals about what is good and what is not. Jesus asked the man to defend his compliment, wondering why he called Him good. Before this man could even vouch for himself, Jesus continued by letting this young inquiring mind know, "No one is good, except God." The problem that this man had, and I also had, was that he was too lost in the paradigm of his doing good to get there. Jesus was guiding the young ruler to look elsewhere than his goodness to go to Heaven, but he was blinded from seeing that. I don't think it would be stretching it to say that during that time, Jesus was by far the best example on earth of what a good man should be like and how a righteous man ought to live. Wouldn't you agree?

If Jesus isn't good, then who is? This young man was very confused, as I would have been too. The first thought that came to my mind is that if Jesus Christ isn't good, then who in the world is? Surely not I. This young man had lived his entire life trying his best to be honorable in the sight of man and God. He intentionally did all of the right things, like following the commandments and obeying the law to the letter. And now Jesus is basically telling this man that his kind of *good* is not *good* enough. It is quite obvious that the *bad* don't inherit eternal life for being *bad*.

So why shouldn't the good people go to Heaven for being good? At first I was as blind as the young ruler. It seemed to be suggesting that there aren't any real benefits to being good. For the most part, even when I wasn't saved, I was pretty much a "good" guy. And although I didn't think that I should get a trophy because I lived my life this way, I still thought that being good mattered, as it rightfully should. But here it appeared at first as if being good really didn't matter at all, not even to Jesus. So my thoughts were, *If being good doesn't matter, then why even bother?* I thought to myself, *Christianity is supposed to be good news? This Jesus guy is flat-out depressing me!*

What should have been a message of hope was God's grace; what He did that would get me focused on my relationship with Him was being twisted into a depressing message. It seemed as if there should be some type of godly benefits that a person gets when they're good, but here Jesus tells a good man in so many words that he cannot consider himself good since no one is good but God. In one moment's time, everything that this man lived for and believed in wholeheartedly had been challenged to the very core. This guy, who had followed all of the rules, and not just any rules—God's rules—had to now totally reevaluate his entire perspective on physical and eternal life.

To me, this said that there is a reward for doing good things, but it is not going to Heaven. Acknowledging Jesus Christ as Lord and Savior is what will get you there, and there are plenty of other rewards for doing good. If you truly believe in Him, you will do well and be good. But the young ruler isn't getting it, so Jesus throws a few jabs to set him up for the knockout punch.

Why Should I Give My Hard-Earned Dollars to the Poor?

Jesus, like a masterful boxer, sets the ruler up. He basically says, "OK, you are looking for something to do? Well, what rules have you followed?" This man must have rejoiced within himself knowing that he was not barred from Heaven, but could enter in on special conditions—conditions that Jesus would clearly lay out. Often Jesus spoke in confusing and complex ways, which caused this young man to be even more baffled after he was given the Master's list of "what to do" (or what *not* to do) to get into Heaven:

- You shall not murder.

- You shall not commit adultery.

- You shall not steal.

- You shall not bear false witness.

- Honor your father and your mother.

• You shall love your neighbor as yourself.

This is basically a shortened version of the Ten Commandments. The young man readily admits that he has kept all of the commandments that Jesus recited. Arrogantly, he does not examine himself in detail at all. He does not ask if there is some layer of complexity to these that he may have missed, he just keeps looking for something new. Confused, he then asks Jesus, "What am I missing?"

This is a question that I have always had a challenge with: "What am I missing?" It seems as if you can do all the right things in life, and yet still miss out on some large or even small element that'll get you thrown right into hell. That really bothered me because it almost seemed like Jesus was toying with this man's life and future. And it's really not fair to play with people's minds.

When Jesus did respond, He delivered a knockout punch by making what seems to be a totally unreasonable demand. Jesus isn't always this blunt with people in the Bible, so why was He with this man? My perspective is that it was because the young ruler was acting like he was perfect. It's dangerous to think you are perfectly following what you know. (Interestingly enough, if you ask most non-Christians, that's how they would describe a Christian!) Jesus told the man that if he wanted to get into Heaven, he should go and sell all of his possessions and give all of the proceeds to the poor.

Take a look at this for a minute. Jesus did not deny that this man had made a truthful confession about obeying the laws his whole life, and He doesn't even question that, almost implying, "I'll give you an A+ in obeying the rules." Despite the fact that he kept all of the rules, there is still one thing that he had to do, and that was give all of his money away to the poor.

Stunned, this man could not understand why he had to give away everything he had to the poor. The Bible says that this man became very sad because he had great possessions. Quite honestly, if I were in his position, I'd be sad too. At the time I first read this, I was actually angry too. Tom, my mentor, had gotten me excited about having nice things, being able to travel, forming new relationships, but now I'm hearing that when I finally get to that point I will just have to give it away? This was getting more depressing the more I got into it!

The more you have, the more you have to lose. This man had great possessions, which meant that he had to give a whole lot away. He had to part with some very valuable wares and give his money away, almost as if he was being penalized for something that he did wrong. When I read this, I couldn't help but wonder if God really hated rich people. To the average Bible reader that's how this whole thing might look.

The more you have, the more you have to lose.

Scriptures like these are the very ones that people use to justify their beliefs against prosperity. If I were anti-prosperity and pro-poverty, I could easily use this Scripture to say, "I told you so. I told you that God hates those filthy rich people. This man was a good rich man, and not even he could get in to Heaven." Since that is obviously the case here, there is really no reason to acquire earthly possessions. Gaining wealth is pretty meaningless, especially since you'll wind up having to give it all away. So the more that you receive, the more God is going to hate you. You are a whole lot better off having nothing, because at least then you won't be judged by an angry God.

OK, I'll admit I'm probably stretching it a bit here, but it's not really hard to see how someone could feel that way. Even if He didn't hate rich people, it really seemed like God got His kicks from playing with people's minds, even the good ones. The list of do's and don'ts had obviously been laid out in front of this man since he was a young child. I'm sure that his teachers taught him not only to do the right things, but also told him that there were great benefits in doing so. No one told this man that there was a secret list, a hidden record separate from the law that one must also do in order to get into Heaven. Had he known about the secret list early on, he would have had the opportunity to find it and incorporate it into his life immediately.

As far as this man was concerned, there was no secret list. Everything that he needed to know, he knew, or at least he thought he knew. Personally, I didn't realize before but have now come to understand that the answers to the questions we have about life are not always written down on pieces of paper, tucked away in a book, or on someone's computer hard drive. Many of the answers in life exist inside of you. Jesus was trying to get this man to discover something about himself that he would have never known until he searched within—*discovering what things really mattered to him the most.* But it is hard to find something when you are looking in the wrong place.

> **Many of the answers in life exist inside of you.**

Ask yourself that question. Do you say that family matters most, yet spend no time with them? How we spend time and money are great truth-tellers. Do you say that God matters, yet you won't share significant amounts of money with Him, only what you feel obligated to? Do you say that growing matters but won't invest in seminars? With the discovery of what things really matter most is the discovery of the key to eternal life. But for some, that discovery may take a lifetime to realize.

GOD PICKS ON RICH PEOPLE

Whether God hated rich people or not, I couldn't really prove in the Scriptures at the time. But what I thought I could prove was that God picked on rich people. In some ways it was a bit confusing since in the Old Testament, God actually caused people like Abraham, Solomon, David, and the tribes of Israel to become rich and freely gave them material possessions and land to enjoy. So I wondered why now, in the New Testament, God went from blessing people with material wealth to condemning people for being rich. This good man, not a bad man, is seemingly being penalized because he is rich. Nothing in the text says anything about this man being a bad guy, a liar, a cheat, a thief, or anything negative. He is a good man faced with having to lose everything in order to make it into Heaven, which seemed pretty severe. For the most part, it appeared as if the poor totally got off the hook, or in some ways were given special favor, for no other reason than that they were poor. NOT SO! God is picking on a rich person here but He picks on poor people in other places in the Bible. He is an equal opportunity God picking on everyone. We all just have different things to work on.

In one case in the Bible, it appears that the poor were penalized for making a bad stewardship decision. There is a parable in the Bible (see Matt. 25:14-30) that deals with three men entrusted with the tasks of properly investing their master's money. Each man was given a certain amount of talents/money to invest. One guy was given five talents, another three, and the other one. The two with higher amounts given to them invested their money and doubled their profit for their master, who was very pleased and ensured them job security for the future.

The servant who was given one talent buried it in the ground and never made a profit. When the master confronted him about it, he began to make excuses and finally blamed his master's harsh and stern attitude as the reason why he was not able to turn a profit. The master, perturbed by this man's blatant ungratefulness and spirit of blaming others, takes the one talent away from him and then gives it to the person who had the most talents to begin with. How many people in today's challenging economy are burying their money and talents?

Now most people would think that this was a wrong thing for the master to do. Why would God approve of taking away from the poor to give to the rich? The answer is quite simple. Many rich people get richer because they follow Kingdom principles that ensure they profit no matter the economic times they live in. Many poor people stay poor because of how they think and their failure to follow Kingdom principles. Giving and seeding is a "Kingdom principle" spoken throughout the Bible. Even when you are down to your last piece of bread or have only a couple fish, you are asked to "give." The person who had only one talent had a mind-set of "playing not to lose" any of the money and did not seed any money to create more money. He paid the price of losing what he was given. I always was intrigued at the end of the story by the talents of the steward who did not invest; thus called "wicked."

Actually, in this parable, it doesn't necessarily say that the person given one talent was poor at all. It does say that the amount given to the stewards (one, three, or five talents) was based on their ability. Perhaps giving according to ability is fairer than simply giving equal amounts. However, the story does strongly suggest that those who don't have as much as others are the victims of the rich in society. Also, poor people tend to make poor stewardship choices just like this man did.

So we have some very strong inferences in this text. Aside from that passage, God appears to make things pretty difficult for rich people to have access into His Kingdom. Today, for the most part, that seems to be the way that many Christians believe. So they choose to live life with far less than they could have—seeing that more riches would only lessen their chances of living with God forever.

Why didn't Jesus ask him to simply give half of his money? Why didn't Jesus ask for 10 or 20 percent? What was Jesus really trying to prove, asking this rich man to fork over everything that he had worked so hard and honestly to acquire? Even today, the mind-set that if you're rich you must be a bad person still prevails in society. For the most part, people in general think pretty badly about rich people. They think that the rich are greedy, have taken advantage of others, and are not as "good" as them. Others are jealous and think the rich are uniquely gifted to acquire dollars, but not themselves.

That's their perspective (what I refer to as their "sunglasses" in my book, *If How-To's Were Enough, We Would All Be Skinny, Rich, and Happy*) on how the rich are. The good news is, that's not true in my experience. The bad news is that society doesn't really care what you think. They're going to think the way that they want to think regardless of the truth. But it really doesn't help living in a world where people inwardly feel that the rich are a bunch of dopes. What's worse is that it seems like God is backing society's viewpoint. I'm not saying He is; it just seemed that way to me at one time.

In society today, many of the richest people are doing the most to help people. Investor Warren Buffet gave nearly $40 billion dollars to the Bill and Melinda Gates Foundation to help children in Africa. Daytime media queen Oprah Winfrey supports more than 100 teenage girls in an all girls' school in

South Africa and has committed to pay for all of their college education in full after they graduate from high school. Media mogul Ted Turner gave $1 billion to the United Nations. So it's really not so bad being rich, especially since the rich are in a position to be able to effectuate great change in society through their generous contributions.

I'm pretty sure that there are just as many poor people who have bad traits, as there are rich who have bad traits. Riches won't make any person bad; they will just magnify what they already are. If you were a compassionate, loving, and kind person before you had wealth, you will only increase in kindness and favor toward others when you get more money. If you were an uncompassionate jerk before you had money, when you get money you will be an even bigger version of that. I think you get the point. So I know that God must love rich people, if only because they can help Him to get His job done on earth.

However, for whatever reason, it appears as if God gets mad at the rich every time He looks at the poor, as if rich people are the reason why the poor are in that situation. Later on as I studied the Bible, I read about plenty of people with large amounts of wealth who still had a great relationship with God, like Abraham, Solomon, and Joseph. However, at first glance it appeared to me that God didn't approve of wealthy people. That whole idea confused me. I knew that I'd rather be on the side of the rich, so I could help more people. But in making that choice, the choice to be rich, one might feel a bit awkward and wonder if that choice was really the best one, especially with regards to how society views rich people.

It's Impossible to Be Saved

In this story, it is rather obvious that good people can't be saved. And even if they could, Jesus publicly announces that no one is good. So that closed off that door. Rich people couldn't be saved unless they gave all of their money away to the poor, but most rich people I know would never do that. It didn't seem to make any difference that some rich people actually followed the commandments, as that didn't work either. So no matter what a person did, it really didn't seem to help the situation of getting them closer to Heaven.

After trying this and that and still all the doors are closed, a person can get really frustrated. You, like this man, may have asked, "I want to go to Heaven, but how will I get there?" Now I know that in life there are infinite ways to get your desired goal. The problem is that the philosophy of *infinite ways* applies to everyday life situations, such as landing the right job, buying your dream home, having an astounding marriage and family life, and even being a massive contributor to every good cause. For those things we can always use the *infinite ways* approach.

Infinite ways doesn't quite work the same when you're a Christian, and it definitely doesn't work with regards to going to Heaven. According to the Bible, there is only one way to get to Heaven and that is through Jesus Christ. Since Jesus is the head of this organization, the founder and CEO, He makes the rules, enforces the rules, and has the power to punish anyone who forgets to obey the rules. Jesus offered no other options, so it really seemed as if this man didn't have any.

The good news the ruler missed is that you don't have to be perfect to get into Heaven! God is, as I heard Larry Osbourne say, "the ultimate come as you are God." The only hoop you and I have to jump through is surrendering to Jesus Christ as our Lord and Savior. That would seem to be a lot easier than being perfect, don't you think? But for many it is not. Even in His knockout punch, Jesus is giving the ruler a way to relinquish control. He is basically saying that you don't have to be perfect to get to Heaven, but if perfect is what you want to pursue, then do this. Then the young ruler in the story collapses.

ANOTHER LESSON LEARNED

One of the things that I have come to accept and know is that Jesus really is a fair and just God. I have to believe that anyone who willingly gave up His life and subjected Himself to the abuse and torture of others could not be all that bad. I used to think that this Scripture was all about God's plan to doom innocent people to hell; I thought it was about how good guys have to suffer. What I came to realize was that this story doesn't only refer to the rich, they're just used here as an example. This story really relates to anybody in life who has something they struggle with letting go of. In other words, can you give up control of your life to Jesus? Wow! This wasn't about money and riches—it was about letting go. Have you ever known someone who had a difficult time letting something or someone go? Jesus would say to a person in an abusive or unhealthy relationship, "Leave that and only then you can enter into the Kingdom."

What are you willing to let go of in order to get into the Kingdom of God? Will you let go of the one thing that is most desirable to you? What is the dearest thing to your heart? Perhaps Jesus was asking us to turn over what is most precious to us (our marriage, our company, or career) to Him and make Him number one in our life and heart. It is not walking away from the marriage or job, but truly placing it in God's hands and looking for His guidance on what to do. So although this parable was about money, it really is about more than money. Some people struggle with a negative attitude. They harbor bad feelings toward others and send out negative emotions toward the people around them. No one really wants to be around them because they make others feel miserable when they come around. When confronted about their attitude, they get angry and defensive, informing everyone that this is just the way they are and they are not going to change. That mind-set, according to this Scripture, will cause someone to miss out on the Kingdom experience.

There are so many things that people are unwilling to let go of. There are millions of people addicted to drugs, sex, alcohol, or even being right. Your addiction can easily come between you and your relationship with God, especially when you doggedly hold onto it. I know of mothers who refuse to let their adult children go. They live their lives through their children. They are always monitoring their adult children and being a busybody and total nuisance. Both the mom or dad and the adult child can't seem to really move forward and make a difference in life, because they are all being sabotaged by an overexposure to one another. They all need to simply let it go!

I have seen thousands of people unwilling to let go of their limiting belief systems and meaningless traditions (discerning from the valuable traditions). I'm not making fun of anyone's beliefs or traditions, but I am suggesting maybe it's time for you to change that thought or practice. Maybe you should let it go. I've heard people credit their parents' or grandparents' abhorrent behavior as the reason they continued in the tradition of self-defeatism. Many people have embraced the generational curse on their own lives for no other reason than they just don't want to let it go. They might not like the limiting belief but they have lived with it and it is comfortable.

Now I do know and realize that letting go of treasured things is not always as easy as it sounds. You have grown attached to that thing you are dependent on. In fact, you have such an intimate relationship with whatever that thing is that you are unwilling to let go of it. Of course letting go will hurt, but the bottom line is that you cannot let go by holding onto the control yourself. You have to allow God to help you in the process. That is why the end of this story reminds us: *With God, all things are possible.* Jesus was trying to get this man to understand a very valuable lesson. Whatever God requires you to let go of, He will strengthen you to be able to do it. God won't leave you hanging. He will help you every step of the way. At one point in my life I was afraid to leave a secure job for starting my own company (which I now believe I was clearly called to do). God has opened innumerable doors and assisted me in that journey. In other cases, it has not been a matter of letting go of my company or marriage but letting go of me having to control it and just allowing Him to guide me.

> **Whatever God requires you to let go of, He will strengthen you to be able to do it.**

So It Doesn't Mean You Have to Do Without

God is not saying you have to be homeless and give everything up. He is saying look to God and see what God wants you to do about anything. What is God telling you to do? Can you trust Him? Look in the Bible and at all the people who had *great* relationships with God and lots of abundance. He wants you to have abundance. John 10:10 says, *"I have come that they may have life, and that they may have it more abundantly."* It's just that abundance is not the end game; it is meant for the purpose of blessing other people.

Early in my career, I was making a good deal of money, but I was naïve. I didn't even have insurance because I thought, *Why does someone doing good need that?* Only later did I learn the biblical principle that "all good is attacked." Someone saw I had the money, and through a series of legal maneuvers they took half a million dollars from me. I didn't let go of money voluntarily in this case, like giving to a charity, but I lost it. He is a God of recovery and so I recovered the money over time. Learning to replace what was lost or given away is mastering Kingdom principles. The faster you can do something, the more of a master you are. Without being so dramatic as giving it all away, may I suggest a forgotten secret called "sacrifice"? I believe when you sacrifice, as in a fast or in giving more money than is comfortable, or a block of time you don't feel you have, you are releasing a spiritual connection to God that opens up wisdom, relationships, and opportunities to you that you would not have otherwise had or seen. It also will assist you in learning to release some control of doing things your way.

> *And everyone who has left houses or brothers or sisters or father or mother or wife or children or lands, for My name's sake, shall receive a hundredfold, and inherit eternal life. But many who are first will be last, and the last first* (Matthew 19:29-30).

Most believers have one entire goal in life—to make it to Heaven. When I first received Christ, I did not understand this concept entirely. I still do not claim to understand anywhere near everything, but I do feel I understand more than I did when I started. Today, I am more mature in God than I was before. Now I know that life is a wonderful journey, not just a fateful passage from an earthly hell to an ethereal bliss. Life is much more beautiful than that, and I intend to enjoy and celebrate life every day while on my way to Heaven. Although many people teach that Heaven is an escape from the realities of earth, I believe that is a limited perception. I believe it's more about bringing His Kingdom principles here on earth. Actually, I look at the everyday fluctuations of life as a prime opportunity to bring pleasure to God by exercising my faith in Him. Also, God takes pleasure when I exercise the ability He gave me to overcome any obstacles that life may present.

A Short Recap

- What you are willing to part with will determine what greater things will come into your life.

- All of the answers that pertain to life are within you.

- You must lose everything in order to gain Heaven.

- God loves the rich, but expects that the rich will love Him more than their wealth.

- Obeying the Ten Commandments alone won't land you in Heaven.

- Whatever you leave behind, God will replace with something of far greater value.

- Heaven is really all about relationships and how you relate with Jesus.

- Jesus really wants you to be in Heaven with Him.

- It's not as hard as you think.

POINTS TO PONDER

1. A great way to see what's truly important in your life—what you really value—is to examine how and where you spend most of your time and your money. For example, do you claim that your family matters most, yet you spend almost no time with them? Do you say that God is your top priority, yet you won't share significant amounts of money with Him or for His purposes? Do you say that growing matters, but won't invest in education, Bible studies, or seminars?

_____

_____

_____

2. Take a minute to make a chart of what your typical day's schedule looks like. Where do you spend most of your time? Does spending time with God and studying His Word have a place of importance in your schedule? What would you like to change about the way you spend your time?

_____

_____

_____

3. Now, take a look through your checkbook register or at past statements of your bank account. Imagine a stranger were to look through your financial records. What things would they assume are most important to you? Do you like what your checkbook says about you? Are you being a good steward of the finances God has entrusted you with?

_____

_____

_____

4. Jesus challenged the rich young ruler to give away all his wealth because He knew that's the one thing that he most treasured and that would be most difficult for him to give up. What is it in your life that you hold onto tightly and refuse to give up for God? Money? Control? The dreams and plans you have for your life?

_____

_____

_____

5. Spend some time in prayer. Ask God to show you how to better steward the time and money He has entrusted you with. Ask Him to help you learn to trust Him completely, even with those things you hold most dear.

_____

_____

_____

CHAPTER THREE

WHY DO GOOD GUYS FINISH LAST?

"*For the kingdom of heaven is like a landowner who went out early in the morning to hire laborers for his vineyard. Now when he had agreed with the laborers for a denarius a day, he sent them into his vineyard. And he went out about the third hour and saw others standing idle in the marketplace, and said to them, 'You also go into the vineyard, and whatever is right I will give you.' So they went. Again he went out about the sixth and the ninth hour, and did likewise. And about the eleventh hour he went out and found others standing idle, and said to them, 'Why have you been standing here idle all day?' They said to him, 'Because no one hired us.' He said to them, 'You also go into the vineyard, and whatever is right you will receive.'*"

"*So when evening had come, the owner of the vineyard said to his steward, 'Call the laborers and give them their wages, beginning with the last to the first.' And when those came who were hired about the eleventh hour, they each received a denarius. But when the first came, they supposed that they would receive more; and they likewise received each a denarius. And when they had received it, they complained against the landowner, saying, 'These last men have worked only one hour, and you made them equal to us who have borne the burden and the heat of the day.' But he answered*" *one of them and said, 'Friend, I am doing you no wrong. Did you not agree with me for a denarius? Take what is yours and go your way. I wish to give to this last man the same as to you. Is it not lawful for me to do what I wish with my own things? Or is your eye evil because I am good?' So the last will be first, and the first last. For many are called, but few chosen"* (Matthew 20:1-16).

I often think of myself as a pretty critical thinker, which is probably why this story caused my thinking to swing from one end of the mental pendulum to the other. At first when I heard this story, I focused on the "unfair treatment" (as I typically did) of the workers. The master was totally unreasonable with regards to how he chose to treat his employees. The strange thing is how easily one person can judge another person when they haven't walked in the other person's shoes.

Arguing with God around this Scripture has taught me that I don't get to pick what's fair and to stop spending fruitless energy in that pursuit. I cannot tell you the amount of anger that has saved me in my life and the sense of depression about life I was experiencing before I was exposed to this Scripture. It has been a frequent source of help in coaching others through difficult circumstances in life.

Before I became a business owner, I would have quickly sided with the employees' point of view and gone running to the labor union to fight against any unfair employer, especially one who showed favoritism toward a select few and paid slave wages to all the others. Now my entire view is different. I haven't changed my viewpoint because I am insensitive and uncaring or because it is simply in my best financial interest to do so. That's not it at all. The reason why my point of view has changed is because I now see things from various angles, not just the angle of the worker.

It is this kind of approach—getting a view from various angles—that causes people to have a better understanding of a situation. Having various ways of seeing things not only provides balance but is also the best way to establish fairness. For example, in some parts of the country, laws that govern property rentals can be pretty strict, favoring the tenant and not the landlord.

Tenants may choose not to pay their rent on time, or even at all, since they know that the law is working in their favor to protect them.

Some tenants may take advantage of this and manipulate the system to no end, until the court finally orders them to vacate the premises. The eviction process could take several months or even more than a year. During that time, the landlord is still responsible to pay all of the expenses related to the property: the mortgage, the utilities, the property taxes, and insurances. When the tenant does not pay rent, where does the money come from to cover all of his monthly expenses? Most tenants do not care about those details.

As long as the deadbeats are allowed to live rent-free, they feel as if they've beaten the system. However, the landlord doesn't think the same way. The landlord sees things from a totally different perspective. Some have actually gone out of the rental business altogether because they could not get the cooperation of their tenants to simply pay as agreed. The funny thing is that the whole scenario changes when the renter becomes an owner of a rental property.

When the former tenant comes to the position of the landlord, suddenly he feels the ride of the pendulum swing that I mentioned earlier. He now has the experience of knowing how it felt to live in both worlds and then having to choose which one of those best fits his liking. The point is that everything in life is all about perspective. It really depends on how you look at things.

Unfair Wages

Let's take a close look at this story. Here you have the master making a deal with his worker that he will pay him a certain amount of money for working his vineyards. For the sake of this illustration, let's just say that this man agreed to receive $40.00 after a full day's work. So then, he began to work for his pay. A few hours later, along comes another man. This man makes a deal with the master to get $40.00 just as the first worker did, but for working far less hours.

The difference is that the second man only has to work one hour in order to get his $40.00 while the first guy has to work the entire day, possibly eight to ten hours, for the same amount of money. Both men agreed to the terms that the owner of the vineyard established. However, the first man became very upset at the fact that the other worker was working fewer hours and exerting less energy than he was, but still getting the same amount of pay.

Most "thinking people" would look at this situation and immediately see the inequity. No matter how you cut it, this seems outright unfair. If two people work equally hard, they should make the same amount of money. And if someone works harder and longer hours, they deserve to be paid more. That's the way that it should be. So the first guy was not being treated fairly. Just think about it for a minute; why would anyone want to knowingly work long hours to receive the same amount of money as a person who only works one hour? That doesn't make sense.

There are millions of people who would view this story as unfair and could easily relate this story to their own life experience. For example, there are many social activist groups attacking Wal-Mart for what they consider to be unfair wages. I don't know enough about Wal-Mart and their corporate dealings to really make the best judgment about whether or not they are treating their employees unfairly, so I dare not judge them. However, what I do know is that many of their employees have filed lawsuits against Wal-Mart, claiming that their unfair practices violate labor laws. They believe that they are being treated unfairly because people in upper management positions generally get paid more than ten times what the average laborer is getting paid. Is this fair? That scenario closely resembles the situation found here in Matthew 20. Even if it is fair, the number of people who believe it is *not* fair is greater than the ones who believe it is.

In California, the new minimum wage is $8.00 per hour. Is paying someone $8.00 per hour fair or should they automatically be paid more money? When you really think about it, wages should reflect a person's work and performance. Some people try to beat the system by showing up at work to do absolutely nothing. For a person like that, $8.00 per hour is a high wage since they're really not earning it. For another person producing far more than $8.00 per hour in production, sales, or quality control, perhaps the wage truly isn't high enough. The point is that a person really shouldn't gripe and complain after they've agreed to accept a certain wage. If you agreed to it, then accept it or work your way above that wage. In life you get what you accept!

Unfair Perspective

In life, how we look at something creates our experience. *As a man thinketh in his heart so is he* (Prov. 23:7). It doesn't change the facts, but it does change our experience of the facts. Recently, one of my sons was in the front row of church and was texting as I was preaching. The worship leader approached my son after the service, feeling angry that he had not respected me. Then my son explained that someone in his franchise had had a diabetic attack while he was sitting there and he was trying to get someone to handle the problem. The facts did not change but the worship leader's experience changed dramatically. Something may appear to one person one way, and to the next as totally different. Concerning this Bible story, my perspective used to be that this master was completely unfair in giving the same amount of money to a person who worked only one-eighth of a full eight-hour workday (in terms of the average contemporary workday). The second man should have gotten one hour's worth of pay, not a full day's pay. That was my perspective back then when I first encountered this verse.

One of the many things that I did not acknowledge is that the master in the story had a perspective about the situation as well. That's what I was missing. I'm quite sure that one perspective he may have had was, "This is my money, and I can do whatever I choose to do with it." Face it, this man did not have to even employ the first gentlemen at all. He could have hired someone else for the job, waited to have the job done at a later date, or found someone willing to work for lesser pay. Then again, he could have simply given his money away.

The owner of this vineyard had several options, but he chose to allow this man the opportunity to work and earn a day's wage. Instead of this laborer being grateful about having a place to work, he adopts an ungrateful spirit by worrying about something that wasn't even his business. His perspective could have been a more grateful one, considering he was given the opportunity to make money. But instead of showing gratitude he voiced his displeasure by saying, *"These last men have worked only one hour, and you made them equal to us who have borne the burden and the heat of the day."*

This man had a voice, and he used it. On second thought, did he really have the right to tell his master how he should spend his money? After all, the master was in the position of being a lord over land because he was probably a good steward and earned that right. This qualified him to make the decision about where he would spend his money or whom he would pay. So whether he gave everybody the same amount of money or not, it did not change who he was.

How he paid his employees was totally his decision, and he would make that decision based on the things that he thought were highly important to him. Most people don't understand that concept. They choose to judge a situation from their limited point of view. When you do this, you'll usually make a terrible mess of things. In all reality, an owner has the right to pay the salary he or she thinks is best with regard to the quality of the work being performed as long as the other person agrees.

Some time ago, I hired a certain man (we'll call him Sam) whom I paid $4,000 a month. Shortly after, I hired another person for the same job (we'll call this one Sally) whom I paid nearly $6,000 per month. One might say that's not fair for the same job. Yet, not only had the market changed, but the second person had prior experience in the network marketing industry, which I was willing to pay additional money for.

Another young man in my company wanted to transfer from inside to outside sales, where he would have a greater ability to increase his income more rapidly. I started him out at $3,500 per month. He was quite a bit younger than the two others that I hired, and not as experienced as they were. So I hired him as an apprentice, seeing that he has potential to become a good salesperson if he works at it. Although I thought I gave him a very generous offer, his spouse (who was my assistant at the time) misinterpreted the offer as being unfair. Having every right to do so, she voiced her complaint to me concerning the matter. I assured her that I was giving her husband a very excellent offer, particularly since he had no prior sales experience. In her mind, she thought that I was unfair and that her husband should be paid the same as the other person.

This parable is about not having your attention on comparing your situation to someone else. It invariably will seem unfair and is a waste of time and energy. Focus your energy on what you want to do, and do that 100 percent and be grateful. That focus will open up more and more opportunities while the first focus will make you unhappy and decrease the opportunities presented.

> **Focus your energy on what you want to do, and do that 100 percent and be grateful.**

What I am trying to convey is that some people choose to live their lives in the victim's chair and are always looking for loopholes to free themselves from responsibility. Each worker made a choice about what to be paid for the work presented. They could have turned the offer down. Perhaps they were afraid there wasn't any other work. It doesn't matter. They chose to do the work for a certain amount of money and that agreement was fulfilled. Blaming anyone is easy but pointless. The real truth is that there is always something people can do in life to change their outcome.

UNFAIR OUTCOME

If a person takes the viewpoint that they can change their life's outcome, they are optimistic and will probably get hired again. If they choose to blame someone, they will be unhappy and probably not easily hired. The real truth is that we can always choose how we look at any situation. When we choose to see where we made choices that impacted that situation, we open up the possibility to make different choices. Can you choose different viewpoints about circumstances you don't like? Unfair outcomes are directly connected to unrealistic expectations. As bad as it is, even a person who was raped can change their outcome if they choose to give a different meaning to their tragedy. What are your expectations in life? What do you believe you should receive in exchange for the pain that you've survived? The problem with thinking about unfairness is that concentrating on it drains you of the energy to create. When that happens, you lose.

Something in life may be unfair, but who cares? Staying in that frame of mind is really not productive. Noted Bible teacher Joyce Meyer tells the story about how her father molested her as a child. Yet she chose a different outcome. Instead of being the victim and feeling hopeless, helpless, and dejected, which would consume all her energy, she became a hope to others who had gone through similar violations. Oprah Winfrey has become a hope to many people who have been raped also. The point is that the outcome we expect becomes unfair only when you have expectations that go beyond your own inner ability. What's obvious about the truth is what's so. What's not so obvious is SO WHAT! A friend of mine, Jim Stovall, went blind in his twenties. He had dreams of becoming an NFL football player. The facts of his blindness were obvious to him and everyone else. What was not so obvious was *so what!* He could make the blindness a big deal or make it nothing. He could make it work against him or for him. The meaning or story we put to the fact is totally up to us. That didn't have to be the end of his productive life. As a matter of fact, he went on to win a gold medal in weightlifting, write several best-selling books, own a satellite television station, and win entrepreneur of the year. He also won the Humanitarian of the Year award along with Mother Theresa and made a Hollywood movie starring actors James Garner and Brian Denehy.

The laborer thought his boss was unfair in this parable because he expected to receive the same amount of money as the others did. His indignation was somewhat justified because he did deserve higher wages but it also wasn't justifiable because he had made an agreement that he was not willing to ultimately accept.

I see this kind of thing happen all of the time in professional sports. You have a guy who accepts a contract for $2 million per year. He is happy with the contract, knowing that $2 million is far more money than he has ever seen in his life. This guy plays two or three seasons, and along comes another rising sports star who lands a $20 million contract with a totally different team, and suddenly the athlete with the $2 million contract becomes jealous and starts demanding more. He begins to think that his contract was unfair, that he was ripped off. His argument is that everyone should be treated the same. If one person gets $20 million, then so should he. But is that really fair?

Should Everybody Be Treated the Same?

For years I thought that everybody should be treated the same. It just seemed right. But really, should everybody be treated the same?

I have three, grown, beautiful children. I love each of them dearly and wouldn't trade any one of them in for anyone else in the world. I believe that each of them knows that. When it comes to giving them money, responsibilities, or even opportunities, each of them is totally different in how they look at those things. Some people would believe that all three children, my daughter, Krystal, and two sons Kelly and David, should be treated totally the same. That really sounds good at first. It sounds like fairness, but it really doesn't make good sense to me.

Each child is different, and I know this. If I expressed my love the same to each one, then probably all three wouldn't feel it. They have different love languages. Each of them has their strengths and weaknesses as well as different life experience. Why would I give all of my children the same amount of money to invest knowing that it might benefit one and overwhelm another? In the story of the talents, not everyone was given the same amount. They were given according to their ability. *That* is a huge lesson. Taking it personally, if we want to be given more, then we need to increase our ability.

As I said previously, I love all my children dearly, but being their father I know how much each of them can handle. Based on that, I would choose the one who will make the decisions most beneficial to what I've entrusted them to do. Everybody, including my children, has strengths and weaknesses. A good father and mother know where to invest the most in their children to get back the maximum return. To treat all of the children the same would really be a disservice to them. They shouldn't be treated the same, because they are not the same. They are different.

Would you give a million dollars to someone who has a proven track record of squandering money? Of course not! That would be a foolish thing to do. *You give according to a person's abilities in life.* However, there are times when you give over and beyond what is required just because you want to show your goodness toward others. That's what I had to realize and accept about this passage. The master paid those men who came at the last hour of the day the same amount of money as he paid those who worked all day long.

OK, that seems unfair. From another perspective this can also be looked at as a lavish display of generosity. If you were on the other end, the receiving end, how would you feel? Would that (being the recipient of the master's generosity) change your perspective just a little? The laborers who were paid a full day's pay for one hour's work must have really viewed the master of the vineyard as an unselfish, loving, and kind person.

His one act of kindness could have easily set up the framework for a strong and healthy working environment, since he was showing his employees how they could expect to be treated if they chose to continue to work for him. I've come to accept the fact that I cannot always explain why God does what He does. One thing that I am confident about is that the things I can't explain about God are never things that are malicious. The things that I cannot explain are usually things that deal with His good character and generosity beyond my scope of understanding.

> ...neither you nor anyone else in the world really deserves God's love, His favor, or forgiveness, yet we get plenty of it every day.

The master wanted to be good, and that's what he did. His goodness was not based on anything that the workers did or did not do. That is a shadow of God's love toward us all. If you wanted to really be honest with yourself, neither you nor anyone else in the world really deserves God's love, His favor, or forgiveness, yet we get plenty of it every day.

I think of myself as a pretty good guy, but in all truthfulness, that alone should not afford me the lifestyle that I enjoy: having three great children, a beautiful wife whom I cherish, and leading one of the greatest personal growth businesses in the world. It would be arrogant for me to believe my goodness warrants anything that I have. Thinking along those lines, was this master really unfair, giving everyone the same amount of money regardless of how much time they put in? I think not. This master was just trying to be like God, always going overboard to display His abundant heart toward His children, whether they deserve it or not.

A Short Recap

- Be happy with what you agreed to. If you agreed to receive a certain amount, don't get bent out of shape if others get more than you. Allow your positive attitude to increase your income earning.

- People don't get to decide what is fair, God does. When humans decide justice, it never works out right. God is the only one who can rightfully determine what's just from unjust.

- People determine how much they are willing to put out.

- The comparison game is always a losing game. There is always somebody faster and always somebody slower. Someone is always smarter, more gifted, and so on. Are you happy with this? If you were happy before, be happy now.

- God is a tremendous businessman.

- Be grateful for what you have.

- Don't judge people!

- God loves all of us the same, but He knows what we should have.

POINTS TO PONDER

1. What was your first reaction when you read Matthew 20:1-16? Did you think, *Hey, that's not fair!* Or did you think, *Wow, what a generous employer!*

_____

_____

_____

2. Is your natural reaction one of justice or of mercy?

_____

_____

_____

3. Do you trust God to know what's best even when something seems unfair from your viewpoint? List some examples from your own life of events or situations that you didn't understand or thought were unfair. In hindsight, what do you think God taught you through those situations?

_____

_____

_____

4. "Based on what you do with what He has already given you, He will determine whether or not you will be chosen to handle more." Sometimes, we humans want God to give us *more, more, more,* when we haven't even been wise in handling the things already in our possession or under our control. If you are faithful in the small things, God can entrust you with greater things. Do you think you are faithful in small things? What things do you need to work on?

_____

_____

_____

5. Spend some time in prayer. Ask God to help you understand the way He sees justice and mercy.

_____

_____

_____

CHAPTER FOUR

IMPOSSIBLE FAITH

And when they had come to the multitude, a man came to Him, kneeling down to Him and saying, "Lord, have mercy on my son, for he is an epileptic and suffers severely; for he often falls into the fire and often into the water. So I brought him to Your disciples, but they could not cure him."

Then Jesus answered and said, "O faithless and perverse generation, how long shall I be with you? How long shall I bear with you? Bring him here to Me." And Jesus rebuked the demon, and it came out of him; and the child was cured from that very hour.

Then the disciples came to Jesus privately and said, "Why could we not cast it out?"

So Jesus said to them, "Because of your unbelief; for assuredly, I say to you, if you have faith as a mustard seed, you will say to this mountain, 'Move from here to there,' and it will move; and nothing will be impossible for you. However, this kind does not go out except by prayer and fasting" (Matthew 17:14-21).

When I first read this I was very excited. You mean to tell me all I need is a little amount of faith and I can make a mountain move?! I am *in!* I wanted that power. I could use it to handle the bills, the problem in a relationship, and maybe in my spare time even do a few good works. Then I began to get depressed. Here are disciples of Jesus who have traveled with Him for three years and they still don't even have a mustard seed to show for it. A mustard seed is so small you can hardly see it, yet after three years watching Jesus do miracles they don't even have that little speck?! Obviously then there's no hope for me. Why would He tell me I could do it and then have such lousy products, like the disciples, as examples of His teaching? Was He a poor teacher or were they miserable students? Then my cynicism grew and I thought, *How come He first tells me that nothing is impossible, yet His next sentence goes "except in this case you need fasting and prayer"? What kind of double talk is that?*

Arguing back and forth with God about what this Scripture really meant has taught me that reason is a great tool but a terrible master. It moved my focus into applying faith instead of searching for it. The elimination of confusion of belief versus faith alone was a major stress reducer. Truly, with a glimpse of what this Scripture meant, I would not have left a secure job to start my own business, write best-selling books, or be married to my wonderful wife. But it started with fighting with God about what He was trying to say.

It was a mental fight. Is this guy Jesus a liar or isn't He? He changes water into wine. He multiplies some fish and loaves to feed thousands. He instantly heals blind people so they can see. He tells me that all these things He does I can do and that faith is the key. What possible motive could He have to tell me that if it's not true? The only thing I could think of was that He was sadistic and wanted me to suffer. But that didn't match anything else in His life. So if it was true, maybe He was telling me I might have to study faith for longer than three years. I was willing to go to college for four years to get a diploma, but would I be willing to put four or ten years into learning faith if I could only move a small hill?

What about you? What effort are you willing to put in? If I had $10 million in my bank account but wasn't willing to study how to withdraw it from the bank, then shame on me. But, I wondered, what if I wasn't smart enough to learn what faith was? Now I had to look to two places: back to the Bible and real people I saw in life.

Looking at the Bible, I found that Jesus was certainly not the only man or woman to use faith to do incredible things. Interestingly enough, many existed previously. Moses parted the Red Sea, which is like moving a mountain. Joshua brought down the walls of Jericho. Gideon beat thousands with only 300 men behind him. Peter might have been a slow learner, but he brought people back from the dead and went from being a fisherman to impacting millions of lives in the way Christianity is thousands of years later.

The Bible is a book, and I know if you are a believer you are shouting, "It's not just a book; it's divinely inspired!" Remember, I am sharing with you my thoughts and struggles as I started my journey. What if it was just stories? I had to check all the angles because I wasn't in faith.

The Bible says that if you have faith, nothing is impossible. That really sounds great on paper, but I didn't see miracle healings as a kid. I saw people in church who struggled in marriages, health, and jobs. Did that mean they had no faith or that they weren't using it? In fact I would read about people who wouldn't take their babies to a doctor, believing God would heal them, but the babies died. That seemed like incredible faith to me.

> **The Bible says that if you have faith, nothing is impossible.**

Later in life I did see miracle healings. Why did it only work sometimes? Did I not know what faith was? A pastor may believe a marriage can be saved, but it ends in divorce. With another pastor, there is a miraculous turnaround. Did that mean the first pastor didn't have faith? And what if I didn't have faith, how could I get it? Was faith the same as belief? How did it compare to a positive expectation? If I truly didn't believe something but acted as if I did, was that faith, courage, or stupidity? I was very conflicted and confused.

FAITH OR OPTIMISM

Before I received Christ, I always looked at faith as a type of positive thinking. I felt that faith was just turning a blind eye to reality. I didn't doubt that there were miracles that happened; I just felt that many people were in a state of denial or were over exaggerating what God did for them. Many years ago, I traveled to the Philippines with friends and checked out some faith healers while I was there. My friends thought that the people claiming to be faith healers were frauds. These faith healers would pull out tumors, cysts, and malignant growths, producing miracles right before my eyes. When someone wasn't healed, they would immediately give explanations. I wondered if I actually saw these things or if it was nothing more than a Las Vegas illusion show.

Let me start off with how the Bible defines faith in Hebrews 11:1: *"Faith is the substance of things hoped for, the evidence of things not seen."* I could see faith being related to hope. People "hoped" to be physically healed or to have more money or to have their children quit drugs. But many people hope and their problems aren't solved, nor can they move mountains. That's only part of the equation. What did the "evidence of things not seen" mean?

Faith is the evidence of things not seen.

First, I tackled the unseen part. Even recently, I have heard Christians describe having faith as trusting that someone will stay on their side of the road or that the plane they get in will arrive safely. To me that is not faith. That's a positive expectation based on experience. Faith is the evidence of things not seen.

I was brought up very reality based. If you couldn't see it, then it wasn't real. Talk was cheap. Yet, I can't see feelings all the time and they are real. So this faith thing is happening in an unseen realm, the spiritual realm, that's as real as the physical world. Maybe it was even more real.

Do I say "I believe" and that's faith? *Webster's New World Dictionary* defines faith as "to trust," "unquestioned belief," or "complete confidence or trust."[1] Quite frankly, that's not faith to me. For many years, people believed the world was flat; they had "complete confidence" or "trust" in that idea. That's a belief. Webster's defines a belief as "a conviction that certain things are true—an opinion or expectation." This belief in a flat world only disempowered the people of that time; it prevented them from sailing as far as possible because they didn't want to fall off the earth.

To me, faith is a complete belief in what is true. *That's a major difference.* Now how do I know what is true? That's the major rub: I don't; you don't. *God does know truth.*

Faith is stepping into the spiritual world and believing from God's viewpoint. Sometimes our particular viewpoints affect what we see, but *not what is true.* God knows the truth, not me; so if I am to have faith I must have a relationship with God to see things His way. A relationship with God who dwells in the spiritual realm is key.

> **Sometimes our particular viewpoints affect what we see, but *not what is true.***

Ultimately two keys for me with faith are: (1) being in a relationship with God, and (2) stepping into the spiritual realm. This is a lot easier said than done, or at least it has been for me. In essence, I have to disregard what my eyes are seeing and my ears are hearing and simply be with God by stepping into His realm.

I have a friend, Pastor John Jackson, who loves to say, "To be a faith person, by definition, you have to be out of your mind." Think about that! Reason and logic are the conscious approaches to understanding faith and God. Most of the world doesn't exist in the reason and logic sphere. Trying to ascertain God with a logical mind can drive you crazy since He can only communicate and be understood through spirit. It became clear to me that I was the one who needed a mind change, not God.

I use a model in our seminars of a three-leveled snowman. Starting at the top, we have a head or conscious mind. The next snowball down is bigger and it is the heart or subconscious mind. These two together are the soul. The third level is what everything rests on—God—who is infinite. The Holy Spirit works from God to the subconscious.

THREE LEVELS OF YOU
1. Head or Conscious Mind
2. Heart or Subconscious
3. God

I was taught to be reasonable and there is value in that, but it boxes you in. Have you ever solved a problem by being unreasonable? I have. And if you insist on being reasonable, you will condemn yourself to living within reason. Reason, like money, is a great servant but a terrible master. It is a tool to be used.

> **Reason, like money, is a great servant but a terrible master.**

In 1977, I moved from Hawaii to California with no promise of a job. I had talked to a company, but they had no openings. However, when I showed up I offered to work for free until they realized they needed me. That makes no sense to the conscious or limited rational mind. But it didn't matter because

I felt a prompting from God and "knew it to be true." I started getting paid about four weeks later and worked for that company for almost 18 years.

In the 1980s, I raised $4 million to construct buildings in honor of my mentor, who was killed in 1983. That made no sense either, because at the time I made less than $100,000 a year and had never raised more than a few thousand dollars. I started with no plan, but I knew in my spirit that it was the right thing to do. I knew that in the "unseen" world God would work through me to make it happen.

The mind can get in the way of our being with God. Beware of being with reason and not with God. That doesn't mean you throw the mind away! It has an important function, but not to solve big problems. Part of its job is to simply distinguish and "choose" what the subconscious should go to work on.

> **The mind can get in the way of our being with God.**

The subconscious or "heart" is way more powerful than the conscious mind. Proverbs 23:7 does not say *"as a man thinketh in his MIND so is he."* It says, *"as a man thinketh in his HEART, so is he."* That's why will power usually doesn't work to stop smoking or lose weight. It *can* work, but most times it doesn't. The conscious mind is like a young boy riding an elephant. The young boy can guide the elephant if the elephant is so trained but the elephant has much more muscle. The subconscious or "heart" holds all our feelings, memories, subconscious programming (like computer software), subjective five senses, and autonomic nervous system (what runs the heart and lungs normally). However, the subconscious lacks the ability to distinguish between reality and imagination. If you imagine eating a favorite food, like pizza, you can get your mouth to salivate. Your body is responding to an imaginary picture because the subconscious mind can't distinguish reality from imagination. The subconscious can also prevent us from being with God. One way that happens is to become so enthralled with how powerful the subconscious or elephant is that we no longer seek God.

Look at the self-improvement industry that I'm part of. There are many seminars offering "how-to" techniques and that's it. That's purely addressing the conscious mind. It's good, but it is only reaching the top level. That's why I wrote my first book, *If How-To's Were Enough, We Would All Be Skinny, Rich, and Happy*.

Some seminars work with the subconscious mind as well as the conscious mind. Using just the mind and subconscious mind is very powerful. You can accomplish way more with the subconscious than you can with only the conscious mind. But that's still leaving out the biggest snowball: God. In fact, some people get so enthralled with the conscious and subconscious that they stop there. That is sometimes called "soul power." The biggest factor in influencing our thoughts and actions is God. Why leave that out? That would be like taxiing a Learjet and being excited that driving it around on the ground is better than walking, but never learning to fly.

Some feelings and beliefs in our subconscious can prevent us from being "aligned with God." That's why I am such a proponent of helping people to become aware of what is in their "heart" and to be able to deal with those things. Some Christians go to church and don't want to deal with their subconscious mind, making transformation very difficult. They don't understand why they can't do what they should. Think of lining up our conscious and subconscious with God as a straight pipeline. When a person is "born again," one of the things they are doing is consciously saying, "I choose to have God (#3) run my life, not my conscious mind." *That is being a faith person.* So although we are calling God #3, after being born again we are making Him #1. In a sense we have flipped the worldview upside down.

I use my doubt to doubt my doubts.

The examples I used above are ones where I lined up with God, no conscious effort on my part. What does a person do when they aren't with God? It's like finding out you have cancer and have only two months to live. Getting out of that situation alive is going to require some mountain-moving faith. Faith in the spiritual realm can produce miracles. While most of us don't see that kind of mountain-moving faith every day, I have seen miracles and that allows me to reject my doubts about faith. In essence I use my doubt to doubt my doubts.

Is "faith" believing against the odds that God will save you? That is an aspect of faith. Look at how the disciples look to Jesus to save them in the storm in the above Scripture. They were saved. But Jesus wants more than that. He gets frustrated with His disciples (and you thought He was calm and never angry?). He says, "Come on, guys. How long do I have to put up with you not listening to Me? You can speak to the wind and the waves in that spiritual realm with faith to rearrange nature. I'll only show you one more time." That's not quite King James version, but that's what the Bible says. And then He shows them. He applies faith by stepping into a relationship with God in the spiritual realm and makes the storm go away. I think that's part of my lesson and maybe even yours.

God wants you and me to step up to the plate and solve our problems by being in relationship with Him and having faith, not take a back seat where we are not involved. (See Mark 9:14-29.) Have you ever been in a relationship with someone where you had to solve all the problems without them? It ruins the relationship. So how can you get in a relationship with God? I don't know of any formula for that any more than I know a formula that works for making a marriage work. You're unique, but obviously there are principles to making any relationship work. You have to spend time together, do things together, talk to each other, and respect and honor each other.

I realized I had a lot of work to do. How much did I really talk to God? How much time did I spend with Him doing simple things like honoring Him? I was pretty good at honoring my wife by speaking positively about her and complimenting what she is great at during every seminar I do and to most people I meet. Was I talking about Jesus and God the same way and as often? Was I not talking to Him because I was intimidated by Him? The good news is, in my experience, He will accept you and work with you however much you want. But you and I need to initiate the relationship.

One of my favorite Scriptures is James 2:26, which says, *"Faith without works is dead."* To me, that means faith is always there for me to use. God is always in the spiritual realm for me to be in a relationship with, so my struggle is to constantly be in a relationship with God while I am at work, home with my wife, out on the golf course having fun, and every other moment of my life. For me, just like most relationships, sometimes it comes easy and sometimes it doesn't. The more connected I am, the more I am able to produce miracles— and yet that isn't the point. Can you imagine someone being in relationship with you, "just to use your power of influence"? Sooner or later, you will realize you're being used and not want to see that person anymore. A leader, such as myself, needs to understand that having everyone aim for the same goal will produce the most successful outcome. Even though people have different opinions, they should be used productively.

Mark 9:14-29 has a story about a boy who would actually throw himself into the water and into the fire due to what appears to be a severe case of epilepsy. His father goes to the disciples and they can't cure him. Then he goes to Jesus and begs for Him to cure his son since that was one of Jesus' main purposes for being placed on the earth. I am somewhat familiar with this disease, because I actually had a cousin who died from epilepsy when he was only 19 years old. During seizures, he would be choking nearly to death and gasping for air. Everybody around would be afraid, not knowing exactly what to do. The few who knew what to do would pray for dear life that what they did would actually work. So I can understand what this man may have thought about the incompetence of Jesus' disciples. The fact that such strong disciples spent time with Jesus and they could not perform miracles was depressing. How could I? Yet later on many people did miracles. So it was not the disciples themselves, it was God working through people performing the miracles. This meant I just had to be a good connector to God and allow Him to move through me. I didn't have to be especially talented; I just had to let God work through me. Could the disciples initially have missed that point?! Based on my experience with my mentor, I can see how they would. Although my mentor kept telling us to go create or solve problems, we often looked to him to bring us to another prison or open a new city because we knew he could do it. That got in the way of seeing we could do it. It took my mentor's death for me to see I could do it. It's interesting Jesus died and THEN the disciples caught on fire. They still had the Holy Spirit with them, but they had to listen and be with the Holy Spirit.

This also keeps me from getting a big head as I give seminars and lead Klemmer & Associates Leadership Seminars, Inc. It's not me doing it. It's simply me allowing the Holy Spirit to work through me. The more I listen to Him, the better I do. Anybody can do that. The object is not to impress people with me, but to help others empower themselves with the same skills. They have the same access to God that I do.

"Nothing will be impossible for you." This is a faith-affirming statement, even for the so-called skeptic. It's clean, direct, and straight to the point. When a person reads it, there is really no shaded area. Either you believe it and act on it, or you just simply reject the whole idea. If you reject the idea, it is not only because you're not aware of what Jesus Christ has in store for you, you also reject it for a totally different reason. It doesn't end there.

The next phrase, *"However, this kind does not go out except by prayer and fasting,"* really puts a damper on the previous. The previous verse says nothing would be impossible, but the next one allows that you may need other things. Which is it? When I first read this I felt conned.

You have probably seen an infomercial before. If so, have you ever actually ordered something from the infomercial? When you are watching the commercial with enthusiastic people demonstrating their wares and effectively marketing all of the benefits associated with the product, you get really excited. Then they offer you something free, a drawing card. The beloved word *free* is that motivating idea that gets people to take action NOW! So you run to the phone and call up the number to get your free bottle of pills, handheld vacuum cleaner, foreclosure online list, or whatever, because it's FREE. What you come to discover is that the company doesn't really want to give you something free, but in order to get it you have to buy something you don't even want. By the time you finish with the operator on the line, if you haven't already hung up the phone, you are pretty frustrated with the whole thing. What started out as being a motivator has now gotten you pretty depressed because they didn't simply do what they said they were going to.

This is how I looked at this Scripture. On one hand, the Bible was trying to get you to exercise faith and let you know that you will receive great rewards for doing so. Since faith is about being with God and seeing things from His viewpoint, then this makes sense. While prayer is obvious, the Bible contains stories encouraging fasting for further inspiration. It is interesting that in modern Western society, fasting seems to be a lost art. It certainly wasn't a part of any training I received growing up. I am talking about consciously giving up food for the purpose of more clearly hearing God (versus going without a meal here and there because you had no money).

So how about it? Do you want to hear God more clearly? Are you willing to commit to a three-day or five-day fast? Pastor Brian Zahn, one of my favorite preachers, has shared with me his use of fasting to more clearly hear from God. During a major transition within his church he went on a 30-day fast and had incredible revelations.

"DOUBTING THOMAS" FAITH

People sometimes say that when you have faith, you won't have any doubts. That's not my experience, but there is a conflict between doubt and faith. Peter walks on water until he doubts, and then he sinks. In a different example, the woman comes to Jesus and asks for help to believe and her son is healed. Faith is not about having no doubt, but rather moving forward in spite of your doubts. When you take a risk, you are doing something despite the repercussions or consequences, good or bad—and that's faith. True faith is always going to require some element of jeopardy.

> **Faith is not about having no doubt, but rather moving forward in spite of your doubts.**

Maybe you think that I was overly analytical in my thinking back then. Whatever you think is fine by me, the point is that there are thousands if not millions of people out there pondering over the same things. God is OK with your doubts; He merely wants to have a discussion (or argument!) with you. Engage Him. What can make our Christian tradition beautiful or ugly is our willingness to grow, or our arrogance in thinking we have God all figured out.

Most of the people operating in the healing ministry or the faith arena can't explain any of the things that happen in their lives and ministries. They simply join with the Scripture that says, *"The Lord has done this, and it is marvelous in our eyes"* (Mark 12:11 NIV). Yet the Bible provides so many contradictions, like that of anger being godly and not godly, that it caused me to question the authority it attempted to establish. There is nothing wrong with questioning God; it can only lead to a clearer understanding of Him and His works. Today, I am more compassionate and I give people more freedom to question and explore the Bible than I would have before. There is value in asking "why" to a story and needing an answer before you can completely understand it.

Part of my whole theology is that I don't know it all. Previously, I thought a bit differently about some things, but it did not make me a bad person or a heretic. It just made me a thinker who had a whole lot of questions. From the bottom of my heart, I believe that Jesus heals people. But I have no physical evidence and can't explain it, and that probably won't happen in my lifetime.

At this point of my walk, there are many things that I just don't understand. Understanding the "why and how" about God is virtually impossible. If you tried to understand everyone around you all the time you would drive yourself crazy, and they're all human—imagine trying to understand God! At the same time there is great value in periodically pausing and reexamining those "why's" so that we are growing and not stagnant.

Trying to understand everything about God is impossible. Simply try to love God and others, while frequently reexamining the Scriptures, and your relationship with God will improve, leading to a better life. If I do that successfully, then I will please God.

Faith may work differently for each person. I can't tell everyone what his or her faith should or should not be. That is why being in a relationship with God is so personal.

FAITH IN ACTION

God is the Healer and He uses people in mighty ways. In faith, we can do mighty things. If you aren't doing miracles, does it mean you aren't close to God? I don't think so. It simply means we aren't using something that is available to us.

Faith is an action word; it's all about producing results. There are a lot of Christians who talk big about God, yet fail to produce any real results. That's a really big turnoff to many people. One of the things that drew me to my mentor was that he was very focused on producing results. In the famous movie, *Jerry Maguire*, starring Cuba Gooding, Jr. and Tom Cruise, Cuba's character, Rod Tidwell, repeatedly said, "Show me the money!" That's how I thought, and in some ways still do.

Jesus preached, but He also showed He could achieve the same things. My mentor showed me how faith works, especially in the business world. I learned the most by observing how he handled the worst business times. Even when we couldn't afford to pay our employees, Tom still encouraged works like donating to charity because he knew that everything would work out in the end. An action like that means we are living by faith. I believe when we take risks or make promises when we don't know how to do something it activates similar to a chemical reaction; faith power that's lying dormant.

Faith demands actions.

Maybe the message in the mustard seed is that we only have a small mustard seed amount of faith, but that is all we need. We must activate it. Miraculously, in the example from the previous paragraph, God brought in the money that we needed in unexpected ways because Tom lived by faith and not by sight. Extreme faith, like that of Tom, made me understand and appreciate the actions of men and women who live by faith. At some point you've got to see results. Faith demands actions.

I am going to love people and trust God. I believe that is my supreme obligation. If I do that successfully, then I will have pleased God.

A SHORT RECAP

• Jesus' students were expected to have the same nature, character, and intentions of their Master.

• Faith is moving forward in spite of your doubts.

• Reason and logic is the conscious approach to understanding faith and God.

• Wrestling with God is not a bad thing at all.

• Genuine faith demands actions!

• If you have never had a fight with God, then you don't know God or the Scripture.

POINTS TO PONDER

1. James 2:26 says, *"Faith without works is dead."* What does that mean to you?

_____

_____

_____

2. "I was pretty good at honoring my wife by speaking positively about her and complimenting what she is great at during every seminar I do and to most people I meet. Was I talking about Jesus and God the same way and as often?" If you are in love with someone, you naturally talk *about* them and *to* them. Do you find yourself naturally talking about God to others, as well as spending time talking *with* God? Or do you talk to your spouse or a close friend more than you talk to God?

_____

_____

_____

3. *"This kind does not go out except by prayer and fasting"* (Matt. 17:21). So how about it? Do you want to hear God more clearly? Are you willing to commit to fasting for a day? A week? Longer if necessary?

_____

_____

_____

4. How does *faith* differ from *belief* or *optimism*?

_____

_____

_____

5. Fill in the blanks: In this chapter there are two keys for faith: (1) being in a _____ with God, and (2) stepping into the _____ _____.

ENDNOTE

1. *Merriam Webster's New World Dictionary.* 2010, s.v. "faith," http://www.merriam-webster.com/dictionary/faith (accessed June 4, 2010).

CHAPTER FIVE

SUPPOSE I JUST FEEL LIKE RESISTING?

"You have heard that it was said, 'An eye for an eye and a tooth for a tooth.' But I tell you not to resist an evil person. But whoever slaps you on your right cheek, turn the other to him also. If anyone wants to sue you and take away your tunic, let him have your cloak also. And whoever compels you to go one mile, go with him two. Give to him who asks you, and from him who wants to borrow from you do not turn away" (Matthew 5:38-42).

There was nothing in this Scripture that I identified with. Everything about this story seemed ridiculous. This Scripture actually painted a very scary picture of the Christian obligation. For me, the practical thing ever since the schoolyard was to stand up for oneself in an argument over anything. I was pretty confident that no one was going to take me out in life without a real major fight. I felt like I was more of a man, strong and confident, when I stood my ground and fought against opposition. If I didn't want someone to do something, then I would just resist and eventually they'd go away. Or, if someone didn't do something I wanted, I would resist so that they would acquiesce. If you didn't resist, you would get pushed around. This Scripture seemed to be telling me to take a course of action that would abuse me and give me the reputation of a softy, a pushover, a person who let everybody run all over them. I wanted no part of that madness.

My fight with God over this Scripture was intense. However, discovering that there was a good resistance and a bad resistance and what the difference was has allowed me to deal successfully with some very difficult circumstances, such as someone trying to steal my business or relatively recently during the economic meltdown having millions of dollars of our reserves frozen in something called auction rate preferreds and still having the business operate. But let's go back to how this Scripture first came across to me.

I tried to put a crack in the Scripture by arguing that maybe it was a matter of degree. Maybe Jesus was saying that with a slap you turned your cheek, but He was not saying that you should let them kill you or your children. Maybe He was saying that you should let them sue you for a cloak, but what about your business or your home? I have actually been wrongly sued for my financial wealth and struggled over this mightily. But if it was a matter of degree, then why didn't He say that?

Here Jesus is giving a new set of really specific instructions on how resistance actually looks. If you ever had a hard time with nonresistance, then you probably think that the counsel Jesus gives here doesn't make sense either. All my life, my thinking has been pretty straightforward. I'm a pretty black-and-white kind of guy. I don't have much room for shaded areas. When the Bible says things that appear to be unclear, not only do I get awfully confused, I begin to resist what it's saying! And then the Bible says in another place like James 4:7 *"Resist the devil."* It was like come on, make up your mind, which is it?!

In Matthew 5 the Bible says, *"If someone slaps you on your right cheek, turn the other cheek and let him slap that cheek senseless too."* Of course I'm paraphrasing and ad-libbing, but I'm sure you're getting the point. I don't know about you, but that makes no sense to me. If someone ever slapped me I would *try my best* to whip him pretty good because that was normal to me. So this verse really challenged the way that I had thought all of my life, forcing me to see the benefit of thinking in the total reverse.

If someone steals my jacket, give him or her my coat too. And if someone forces me to run a mile, I should willingly run two, even though I didn't want to run the first mile. Why would Jesus ask people to go to such extremes to make a statement? It didn't really appear to me that these Scriptures helped a person build courage and character. In many ways, I thought that these Scriptures produced cowards, punks, and weak people. There had to be a deeper meaning to all of this.

I was totally clueless, but if I was going to continue searching for meaning and understanding in life, I would have to come to grips with Jesus' motive for introducing this radical concept. Although I wasn't the most open-minded person in the entire world, I wasn't the most close-minded either. No one I knew was really following this Scripture in his or her day-to-day life so I looked at history.

I was born in 1950, during the period of history when Martin Luther King, Jr. stepped out onto the world stage and made history. I listened to his speeches and read about his nonviolent approach. He certainly had courage and repeatedly put his own life in danger and yet was still a force to reckon with. The situation was violent, but he and his followers were not. This began to give me a different understanding of what Jesus was trying to communicate. Martin Luther King, Jr. was certainly no weakling. I have to confess, I also read Malcolm X and he seemed more my style at the time. His style seemed to be, "Don't pick a fight, but if someone else starts one, just make sure you finish it."

Martin Luther King was radically different—almost the reverse. He would pick a fight, but not use violence. I saw he had studied Mahatma Gandhi, another proponent of nonviolence who freed one of the largest countries on earth from the strongest military power at the time, without violence. It intrigued me. Later on, I studied certain martial arts like Aikido, where you were obligated to protect yourself and the attacker. What an interesting notion!

This didn't answer all my questions about this piece of Scripture, but it gave me an opening. So a key to understanding "nonresistance" is that it *does not* mean resigning or giving up. It *does not* mean being passive or allowing oneself to be a doormat, and this alone was a huge insight or revelation.

RESIST NOT EVIL!

Society teaches us to believe that we have to resist for our very survival, in order for us to stay in control. Think about it. Don't you have self-talk (where the conscious and subconscious are talking to each other) that says "if somebody pushes on you then you have to push back to survive"? That's resistance. So a decision is made by management or our pastor that we don't like and we are pushing back by talking negatively or simply not doing what we are asked to do. I came to realize this is a *false* belief. False meaning resisting doesn't help us survive. It causes us to lose control. In our personal mastery or quickening seminars (www.klemmer.com), I go through a whole teaching on this and then have someone sit in a chair and put their hands up. Our facilitator will slap the person's hands; invariably the person pushes back. Can you visualize this? The person in the chair tips backward. When we resist, we actually lose control, but our belief is saying we have to resist for control. There actually is an old adage that what we resist, persists. We actually make things worse or prolong the problem with our resistance. We believe our resistance will change things (stock market dropping, our spouse's bad habits, or any number of things). It doesn't. Not resisting does not mean do nothing and be passive. Think of certain martial arts where you don't push back (resistance), but you protect yourself by stepping out of the way, and then actually use the force against you to put them on the ground. This I believe is what Matthew 5:39 is talking about. It doesn't mean do nothing and let evil take over. Ghandi has become synonymous with non-resistance and he used this Kingdom principle (even though he wasn't a Christian) to overthrow the most powerful nation on earth to free India.

This, I believe, is the Kingdom principle Jesus was teaching. What is it that you are resisting? Society shows us how to resist by putting up a wall and cutting off communication. It gives us the blueprint and instruction manual. Jesus teaches people just the opposite, how *not* to resist. He knows that resisting is really the beginning of a long, self-defeating process. So, it's better to avoid going down that road altogether.

Quite often, I use this text when I am teaching what I call the three R's: resentment, resistance, and revenge. Most people in the world resent when things don't go their way. Then they resist. Next, they attempt to get even or have revenge. When this happens, it is *always* a self-destructive decision. The worldview is that you have to resist in order to be in control, and that is why most people resist everything. It's why people resist change, although it never works.

> **...accept evil for what it is and instead of pushing directly back, step out of the way and turn its punch on itself.**

The world today is in great economic upheaval and change. It is not the change that will hurt most people, but their resistance to it. Jesus was teaching a Kingdom principle to assist us in leading an abundant life. Again, nonresistance does not mean we throw our hands up in the air and say, "Oh well, what will be, will be." That's resignation. Think of Martin Luther King, Jr. It means accept evil for what it is and instead of pushing directly back, step out of the way and turn its punch on itself.

That is why the whole subject of forgiveness is so meaningful. Forgiveness helps people avoid the dangers of resisting. No matter who you are, when you resist, you begin down a spiraling path to nowhere.

Being in resistance sets you on a path to become vengeful and hoping that other people experience harm, especially if they have harmed you. It all starts off with resentment, a negative emotional reaction or response to what we believe someone has said about us or done to us or some other person. Everybody has daily exposure to situations that can potentially lead to this reaction, whether they are instigated by family members, coworkers, husbands, wives, or simply people we see on the street.

For example, husbands and wives may resent each other at times due to a lack of appreciation or love for the small things that they do daily. Children may perform poorly in school and cause a parent to become resentful, especially when they have made personal sacrifices in order for their child to have the best education. A pastor of a church may have been totally misused and taken advantage of, causing him to resent pastoring. There are so many different scenarios. The point is that when something happens in life and you cannot understand why, you open up the door to resentment.

The Bible says that it is normal to get angry or be resentful. Ephesians 4:26 says, *"Be ye angry and sin not"* (KJV). It is unrealistic to expect that you can live a life where children die, loved ones suffer in pain, people have affairs, or someone simply cuts you off in the church parking lot and not get upset. But it's not OK to stay there. In other words, go ahead and get mad because it's normal, but don't stay there and handle it so you don't miss the mark. As I read the Bible, God was one of the angriest characters. He got mad at Sodom and Gomorrah; He got mad at Aaron and the people when they made the golden calf. He got mad at Moses for not doing what He told him. Maybe there are actually times when we should get mad. But bitterness or holding onto that anger (see Heb. 12:15) is self-destructive. It even talks of righteous anger, but without sin. Sin is an old archery term referring to missing the mark or the bulls-eye. Perhaps what the Bible was saying is that it is normal to get mad, but don't stay mad because that will destroy you. It will mess up your aim and you will miss the mark.

However, the average person won't let the anger go and will slip into resistance. Resistance is saying, "It shouldn't be this way." It is a denial of reality, and we begin putting up a wall and cutting off communication. In resistance, you refuse to give anything of yourself, fearing that the other person may want to take too much and leave you with nothing. If resentment and resistance went no further than that, it would be harmful enough. But this cycle always seeks to complete itself by descending to the final and most self-defeating stage: revenge.

Getting Revenge Feels Great!

Many people who feel they've been used, abused, mistreated, misunderstood, and misinterpreted seek revenge. Revenge does feel great in the moment. That's part of why we do it. People who say they've been hurt often respond by doing more damage than the original offender, because they seek to destroy them by any means. Revenge is an attempt to get even at someone. We do hurt the other person, but what we miss is that we get hurt in the process also. The act of revenge can waste years of opportunity, exhaust all our energy or creativity, leave no room for new relationships or businesses, and it never ends well.

Donald Trump is a man whom I admire for his business smarts and profit-making skills. However, even though he is a great businessman and probably a good person, there are some things that he may find beneficial to move away from in his own personal life. One area that he has not conquered is the area of "letting go" when people try to hurt him. He adamantly believes in getting revenge and will quickly label you a "schmuck" for not wanting the same. In his book, *Think Big and Kick Ass (his words not ours) in Business and Life,* with Bill Zanker, he dedicates and titles an entire chapter to this idea of revenge. Trump says:

> So do not hesitate to go after people. This is important not only for the person you are going after but for other people to know not to mess around with you. When other people see that you don't take crap and see you are really going after somebody for wronging you, they will respect you. Always have a good reason to go after someone. Do not do it without a good reason. When you are wronged, go after those people because it is a good feeling and because other people will see you doing it. Getting even is not always a personal thing. It's just a part of doing business.[1]

Far be it from me to judge Mr. Trump, especially since this is exactly how I believed for many years of my life. Much like resistance, revenge seemed right to me. I mean if someone started trouble with me, then it would only seem natural for me to finish them off. "If you don't want trouble, then just leave me alone," that was my motto. If you started a fight with me, I was determined to beat you down so badly that everybody would know not to ever mess with me.

So I understand why Mr. Trump thinks like he does, because it seemed to work and definitely makes you feel good in the moment. But is it a short- or long-term solution? Did it work for Donald in his marriages? Has it worked with labor unions and management? How about in the Middle East where the "three-R cycle" has gone on for centuries? Because what happens when a person has revenge done against them? They get revenge back or their families get it for them, and the cycle perpetuates itself. What I didn't realize then is that the process was not only self-defeating but many times unending. Once we have revenge then someone seeks revenge back. Now we must get more revenge. In some ways it seemed as if that kind of thinking attracted fights to me, even if I wasn't looking for one. By the time you've reached the revenge stage, logic goes out the window. It's all about getting even. That's what revenge is: Getting even. Are there ways to protect yourself from evildoers or abusive people (which there are in business) without getting even? I believe there are although it is not always easy to see.

People usually shut down emotionally at the resistance stage and close off all communication. Unfortunately, without communication you can never make the necessary steps toward progression and establish a new and better direction for a relationship. Usually once a person is at the revenge stage, you cannot convince them to stop. They're out for the kill. I remember how I used this destructive tool of revenge in my own life, especially during my military service years.

The difficult part often is seeing how to stand up for oneself and not seek revenge simultaneously. Shortly after I was first exposed to this whole notion of nonresistance I received a test, like so many followers of Jesus. In the mid-1970s, I was in the military, but I had already put in my resignation. As an S-4, in charge of various logistics including an ammunition depot, my job was to be accountable for what was in the bunker. The guards on duty at the bunker, led by a Sergeant Major, slept and even smoked dope on the job. I asked my boss, the Lieutenant Colonel, to give me authority over the guards so that I could address and deal with this problem before it got out of hand.

The Sergeant Major did not believe that it would be beneficial to his command to give me authority over his people. One day there were some 81-millimeter mortars that were stolen, a major incident requiring a congressional investigation. The Lieutenant Colonel, in order to protect his job, decided to use me as a scapegoat and blame me for the problem. In his mind, there was little harm done because I was already leaving the Army. I was hurt and very mad because it wasn't fair or right. I was in the first stage of the three R's: resentment. If I didn't change my path quickly, I'd be well on my way into resistance and revenge. But I had started to work on this notion of nonresistance and I could clearly see how revenge would in fact hurt both of us.

My problem at the time was that I didn't fully understand nonresistance and I interpreted it as being passive. So I did not speak up for myself and got taken advantage of more than necessary. In hindsight, there was much I could have done to speak up for myself without trying to take other people down.

OUT OF THE BOX OR OUT OF YOUR MIND?

"You have heard that it was said, 'You shall love your neighbor and hate your enemy.' But I say to you, love your enemies, bless those who curse you, do good to those who hate you, and pray for those who spitefully use you and persecute you, that you may be sons of your Father in heaven; for He makes His sun rise on the evil and on the good, and sends rain on the just and on the unjust" (Matthew 5:43-45).

This didn't make sense to me. Why would anyone in their right mind want to love their enemy? And what sense does it make for you to be a blessing to some jerk who keeps cursing you? That would be like loving Osama bin Laden today!

> **Why would anyone in their right mind want to love their enemy?**

I used to have a "take them all out" attitude, ironically similar to that of Osama's. I began to experientially and philosophically explore my connection to every human being on the planet. Like two islands appearing separate above the water but below are connected, all the things that separate us—like our bodies, where we live, our political affiliation—are above the water line. Yet we are told that we are all parts of the same body. Somewhere at a level we cannot see with our eye we are all connected. Jesus said the biggest commandment was that there is only *one* God and that we should love Him with our whole heart and soul (see Mark 12:29). The second biggest commandment was to love your neighbor as yourself (see Mark 12:29-31). I had to look at resistance and revenge in a whole new light. Part of the challenge is that a single word can mean several different things. In English the word "love" could mean the love a parent has for a child or the love that exists romantically between a husband and wife or the love one has for a sunset. This helped me get over the confusion of being told in Matthew 5:39 not to resist evil and then in James 4:7 being told to resist the devil. Let's look at the resistance in Matthew 5:39 as pushing back or cutting off communication versus the resistance of James 4:7 as "overcoming."

If I resist your punch, then I am stuck to you. *What you resist will persist.* So when Jesus said to resist not evil, He was actually giving you the formula for winning over evil in life. Resisting evil will only cause you to become overtaken by it, surrounded by it, and engaged in it. The way to overcome evil is not to resist it but overcome it with good. Go the extra mile! Go beyond the expectation of your enemy or the person with whom you are in resistance. When you do this, you win and the other person does too. *Do not be overcome by evil, but overcome evil with good* (Rom. 12:21).

THE MANY FACES OF RESISTANCE

Resistance 1 a: an act or instance of **resisting; Opposition b**: a means of **resisting; 2**: the power or capacity to resist: as **a**: the inherent ability of an organism to **resist** harmful influences (as disease, toxic agents, or infection) **b**: the capacity of a species or strain of microorganism to survive exposure to a toxic agent (as a drug) formerly effective against it.[2]

If resistance came in one kind of package and looked the same way every single time, then it would be rather easy to identify and you could easily destroy it when it showed up. Unfortunately, it is not that easy. Resistance is a multi-faced monster. It has many disguises, comes from different directions, and its reason sounds very different each time. One of the ways people can become confused as to whether or not they are in resistance is when they look at it as only one mechanism, like not talking. That is resistance—cutting off communication or putting up a wall—but it is just one way of doing the type of resistance we are talking about.

There are many ways that resistance shows up in your daily life. I am here to help you identify some of the various disguises that resistance wears and to assist you into seeing that it is not harmless. When you resist (put up a wall or cut off communication), your resistance always does damage and the worst damage is usually to yourself. Remember that! Learning to separate that definition of resistance from the resistance as "overcoming" spoken of in James 4:7 is important. So let's recognize how to avoid the trap and quickly identify this self-defeating behavior, no matter how or when it shows up. Let's take a look:

Shoulds and judgments are ways of resistance. When a person lives their life always saying that something should be this way or that way, rather than simply accepting it for what it is, that is a form of resistance to reality. For example, a person might say that they should have more money by this time in their life, and by staying in that frame of mind they actually resist having the money they desire. Also, when a person continually talks about what *should* be, that could lead them to become judgmental, which of course is another form of resistance. What might you be in resistance to? Perhaps your spouse won't attend church with you or you are 20 pounds overweight? One of the penalties of resistance is that it robs you of joy. I *want* to make lots of money is different than saying I *should*. We think resistance will change someone or something and it rarely does. In fact it uses up time, energy, money, creativity, and frequently prevents us from finding the way that could change the situation. Accept reality for what it is, whether it is the stock market going down or a child's misbehavior, and then work on the appropriate response to get the result you are looking for. When you do that, you are no longer in resistance and you open the door to allow God to work wonders in your life.

Resistance is putting up a wall or cutting off communication. So many people close off communication with a person they have been involved with as a form of protection from more hurt or harm in their lives. Sometimes they cut off communication to send a message to the other person that they are in control, or maybe they are punishing the other person. Whatever the reason may be, when you cut off communication you are in resistance and as a result you receive all of the negative trappings that go along with it. The Dead Sea receives the river Jordan but doesn't give back to any other body of water and that is why it is dead. This is what happens when people cut off communication from a person. Whatever is on your heart is better openly and honestly expressed to a person than just shut off. Even if the person does not respond the way you think they *should*, that really does not matter. The objective is to not be in resistance. Speak your heart. Ultimately you are not really doing it for them but yourself.

"It isn't supposed to be this way" is resistance. Have you ever heard someone harp about how something is supposed to be? I have, and it is not very consoling. I'm guilty myself of resisting in this way. This kind of resistance happens with people who are especially strong-willed individuals. Although they are determined go-getters, they can, at times, lose out big in life because of their insistence in things being the way they are supposed to be.

This is one area that I have a real close connection with. At 45 years old, I had to start all over again. At this time, I had worked for a company for 15 years and thought that I should have held a senior position in the company with a pension by then, but that's not what happened. Thinking this way made the situation worse. The bottom line is that everything in life is not always going to happen the way you think, and that is all right. Things don't always work according to your plan in order to work for God's master plan. God in His sovereign power has a plan and purpose for your life. Sometimes that plan is not as easily recognized at first, but will reveal itself in time. Don't resist just because things are not working out the way they are "supposed to." There is a saying that goes, *"Let go and let God!"* The moment that you let go of the wheel and stop trying to micromanage everything around you is when God will begin to steer things in the right direction. Be flexible!

Some people ask, Why me, God? In life you have to ask the right question if you expect to receive the right answer. Some people ask, *God, why me?* I've been there myself. When I got wrongfully sued and had to pay out big bucks to a total liar, I wanted to know, why me? Really, that was the wrong question. In this form you never get the solution you desperately need. Your questions keep you from moving forward. You never do anything about your problem because you are spending all of your energy trying to figure out why it happened to you. Instead, acknowledge it for what it is, and then *choose* to accept that God has allowed this to happen to you so that He will get glory through your miraculous healing, or that it will grow you in a way to reach a bigger dream or something else that moves you forward. Even if that were not true, you can now move forward. Resistance costs you time—time you could be using to find a way out.

An amazing example of how not to resist was done by Mr. Lance Armstrong. Mr. Armstrong won the Tour de France seven consecutive times, from 1998–2005, despite the fact that he had been diagnosed with testicular cancer. Armstrong looked for ways to discover how he could beat this cancer and stay on course with his life goals. Despite the cancer, the chemotherapy treatments, and all of the mental and emotional fluctuations associated with this disease, he didn't go into the self-pity that resistance would have caused. This literally slingshot him into good health and seven championships. Armstrong began looking at his battle with cancer as something that would cause him to win big in life. He said in a magazine interview:

> Without cancer, I never would have won a single Tour de France. Cancer taught me a plan for more purposeful living, and that in turn taught me how to train and to win more purposefully. It taught me that pain has a reason, and that sometimes the experience of losing things—whether health or a car or an old sense of self—has its own value in the scheme of life. Pain and loss are great enhancers.[3]

Now, contrary to what he may believe, my view is that cancer really did not teach him anything. It was his nonresistance to it that allowed him to learn the lesson. Armstrong chose to create and define great lessons from his struggle with cancer. Because he chose not to resist, he won—and so will you.

Salespeople resist rejection and then lose the prospect. Rejection is a part of life. It is as natural as waking up in the morning and going to sleep at night. However, a lot of people have a hard time with rejection. They resist it. They take it personally and just back down from opportunity in life. When that happens they lose their prospects. Life is really a numbers game. You lose some and win some. You really won't benefit by resisting rejection.

Remember earlier when I told you that what you resist would persist? If you are really trying to turn things around in your business life, stop viewing rejection as a bad thing but as the very thing you needed to win in the situation. There is a sales technique that uses nonresistance to objections called the *Three F's: Feel, Felt, Found.* Let's say someone gives you the objection that they can't afford something. You don't say, "Yes, you can." That's resistance and you lose the prospect. You reply, "I know how you *feel*, I have *felt* the same way, and what I *found* out is that if the return is high enough, we can find the money to invest." If they still are stuck and can't afford it without resistance, you move on to someone who will be interested and willing to explore how to pay for the value. You will gain more customers by saving the energy in forgetting the customers who do NOT see your opportunity. My thought is that there are millions of prospects in the world, and if one person doesn't want to listen to what I have to say, then there are millions more who will.

Procrastination is resistance. This is a big one. If there is one sin that everyone in the universe has been guilty of, it's this one. Procrastination is simply this: you have something that needs to be done but you put it off. You would rather be comfortable now and deal with the consequences of your inaction later. It always catches up with you. Procrastination makes you lose the deals. It makes your integrity questionable as people tend to judge you when you put off doing what needs to be done now.

Everybody does it from time to time. Overweight people procrastinate by not doing anything about their weight situation even though it could cause serious health complications in the future. Trust me, I'm not judging you at all; I've been guilty of it too. There have been many times I knew that I was supposed to be working out, but procrastinated and used the excuse of "being too busy" as my crafty alibi. You can see here that resistance is damaging, as it keeps you in the place that you started. When you are in resistance, you don't grow.

There are many other forms of resistance, far too many for me to actually list here. Denial is a form of resistance, as is confusion, or feeling guilty. My dear friend Azim Khamisa had a son who was shot and killed because of gang violence in San Diego. Mr. Khamisa forgave the young man who killed his son and even reassured the young man's family. More than that, Azim Khamisa started a foundation that helps urban children on a national level end violence amongst youth. He teaches nonresistance in a practical way to street kids. Check him out at www.tkf.org.

His foundation is doing well and helping to change the lives of thousands of young people who would otherwise find themselves in the justice system. Suppose Mr. Khamisa allowed himself to feel guilty about what happened to his son. He could have easily thought, *My son would probably be alive if I did not expose him to this area. Maybe we should have been living in Bel Air or Beverly Hills. I'm such a bad father for allowing this to happen.* Instead, he did not resist and found answers and solutions to a much larger problem.

> **Clarity is the opposite of confusion, so seek it in all situations.**

Confusion. This happens when you resist understanding. If you do not understand, then you will not have to take action. This happens in corporate America all of the time. Clarity is the opposite of confusion, so seek it in all situations.

Denial. Some people deny that they have health challenges. People deny problems in the areas of money, marriage, health, and spirituality every day. Denial doesn't help. It helps you feel short-term comfort but does no long-term good. Denial makes you feel as if you don't have to pay the price for knowing. If you are denying that there is a God, then you don't have to deal with the price to pay in that moment.

Apathy. Have you ever heard the phrase, "Sticks and stones will break my bones but names will never hurt me?" In order to avoid the pain, I put Novocain on the hurting area but the pain is still there. Just because you temporarily can't feel it, doesn't mean that it is not there.

THE CURE

Let's be totally honest. From time to time, I still struggle with resistance. I don't know if anyone in the world will ever fully conquer resisting, but the goal is to minimize it. Another goal is to recognize when you are in resistance and quickly correct it. Finally, you must be fully aware of what it causes you to lose. Is there a complete cure to resisting? I'm sure there is, but most people would probably not follow the prescription. I believe the best cure is to be conscious of your actions on a daily basis, and when you feel like resisting, think first and change your actions for a different outcome. Ask yourself:

- What will I gain from resisting?

- More than that, what will I lose by resisting?

- By not resisting, are there doors that may open for me that otherwise would remain closed?

- Do I really want more of what I'm resisting?

Know what resistance looks like. I've shared several examples of what resistance looks like and a summary so that you can avoid it.

Resistance looks like this:

1. Denial

2. Confusion

3. Judgment

4. Procrastination

5. Resignation

6. Anger

When you find yourself entering these areas, you will know ahead of time that it is resistance and that it will lead down a very deadly path. So take a different road and bypass some avoidable traps. Do these three things and you will find the beginning of your path toward healing, releasing, and moving on:

1. Forgive

2. Give

3. Open, honest, responsible communication

A Short Recap

- What you resist, you persist.

- Resistance hurts you more than anyone else.

- Resisting is a self-defeating process.

- Forgiveness frees you from the toxic side effects of resistance.

- Revenge may feel great but is a never-ending cycle.

- The thing that you are resisting may be the greatest teacher you've ever known.

- Protect your opponent and protect yourself. Don't seek to destroy anyone.

- Overcome evil with good.

Points to Ponder

1. Search your heart and see if you are currently progressing through the three R's: resentment, resistance, and revenge. Write down what you are struggling with and ask God to help you release it into His care.

_____

_____

_____

2. "The moment that you let go of the wheel and stop trying to micromanage everything around you is when God will begin to steer things in the right direction." Do you find yourself holding on so tightly to the steering wheel of your life—out of fear, lack of trust, desire for control, etc.—that God is unable to guide your path?

_____

_____

_____

3. Explain the sales technique called the "Three F's: Feel, Felt, Found." How does this apply to you as a Christian?

_____

_____

_____

4. According to this chapter, if you do these three things you will find the beginning of your path toward healing, releasing, and moving on: (1) _____, (2) _____, and (3) _____.

_____

_____

_____

5. "The thing that you are resisting may be the greatest teacher you've ever known." Can you think of something specific in your life that you've been resisting? Do you think that God might be trying to use this issue to help you grow?

_____

_____

_____

ENDNOTES

1. Trump, 192.

2. *Merriam Webster's New World Dictionary*, 2010, s.v. "resistance" http://www.merriamwebster.com/dictionary/resistance (accessed June 4, 2010).

3. American Transplant Foundation. http://www.americantransplantfoundation.org/creativecoalition.htm (accessed June 4, 2010).

CHAPTER SIX

GOD SHOWS FAVOR TO SNEAKY SCHEMERS

Once when Jacob was cooking some stew, Esau came in from the open country, famished. He said to Jacob, "Quick, let me have some of that red stew! I'm famished!" (That is why he was also called Edom.)

Jacob replied, "First sell me your birthright."

"Look, I am about to die," Esau said. "What good is the birthright to me?"

But Jacob said, "Swear to me first." So he swore an oath to him, selling his birthright to Jacob.

Then Jacob gave Esau some bread and some lentil stew. He ate and drank, and then got up and left.

So Esau despised his birthright (Genesis 25:29-34 NIV).

To steal from your own brother is bad enough, but to do it when they are desperate? That is harsh, underhanded, and selfish. Why in the world would God want to promote the wicked brother? Esau gets no points either. I mean, yes, he was very hungry, but he certainly wasn't on death's bed with starvation. So he either didn't value the birthright or he had no intention of keeping his promise. And it just gets worse. Jacob then deceives and lies to his father to unrightfully get the blessing.

> *Jacob went close to his father Isaac, who touched him and said, "The voice is the voice of Jacob, but the hands are the hands of Esau." He did not recognize him, for his hands were hairy like those of his brother Esau; so he blessed him. "Are you really my son Esau?" he asked.*

> *"I am," he replied.*

> *Then he said, "My son, bring me some of your game to eat, so that I may give you my blessing."*

> *Jacob brought it to him and he ate; and he brought some wine and he drank. Then his father Isaac said to him, "Come here, my son, and kiss me." So he went to him and kissed him...* (Genesis 27:22-27 NIV).

Why in the world would God be promoting such a jerk? Jacob lies to his father who is physically weak and incapable of catching him in a falsehood. Was God trying to say that the ends justify the means? If Jacob got away with stealing some small blessing, that would have been bad enough; but he got away with the entire inheritance that was designated for his older brother. For whatever reason, God seemed to think that nothing was wrong with this at all. If He did, He never voiced His opposing feelings openly. That made me believe that God didn't have a problem with schemers, and in fact, they may have had His approval. This had to be one of the most confusing and convoluted stories I read in the Bible.

However, in my fight with God over this Scripture, it was one of the key pieces that made it OK to fight with God; it clued me in that I had to listen to God as I fought with Him and struggle to see the way He might be looking at things. It has given me the patience to be in the fight for the long haul as I have grown our business. It taught me a valuable lesson that my past did not have to determine my future. These lessons helped me go from being unsuccessful in relationships to celebrating 26 years of an incredible marriage.

The story, however, started off seemingly absurd and became more and more complicated; full of deception, lies, and corrupt personal relationships. You see the father, Isaac, had lied to the Philistines by telling them that his wife was really his sister, just to save his own skin. So much for chivalry! He'd rather they make sexual advances on his wife or actually sleep with her, rather than be harmed himself. But later on he sees he was deceived by Jacob, yet he still feels obliged to honor the fact that he promised the blessing. The mother, Rebekah, is no better either since she is the one who aided in the deception by Jacob.

After lying to his father, Jacob works extremely hard for seven years to win Rachel, the woman he desires to be his wife. That's pretty noble. Then he is deceived by Laban, who gives him the wrong daughter as a wife. How could Jacob not have realized that the woman he was sleeping with was not the right one?! But then, because he really loves Rachel, he agrees to work another seven years to get her as a wife too. He keeps that promise. But then the two wives become competitive with each other, producing children only to receive love from Jacob and even offering him their maids as sexual companions. And Jacob goes along with it!

Robert Southey (1774–1843), an English writer and poet, once wrote:

> All deception in the course of life is indeed nothing else but a lie reduced to practice, and falsehood passing from words into things.

God doesn't necessarily see things the way that you and I do, but nonetheless He is still just. Although we may believe that certain actions warrant certain results or consequences, these decisions may be made based on our own personal views or opinions. However, God loves all of us equally and can make the correct and righteous decision that will benefit everyone. King Nebuchadnezzar knew that God was a just God and spoke of it in the Book of Daniel.

God doesn't necessarily see things the way that you and I do

Now I, Nebuchadnezzar, praise and exalt and glorify the King of heaven, because everything He does is right and all His ways are just. And those who walk in pride He is able to humble (Daniel 4:37 NIV).

What a lofty compliment to give anyone! All of His ways are just. But how did that play out in this story of Jacob? God is a just God. But His justice is not always easily perceived. He seems to have a different standard to gauge justice by than we do in our own society. God pardons the wicked and also those who have evil thoughts. To me that didn't seem right, but I was trying to look through God's eyes or viewpoint. To me, if someone was wicked or had evil thoughts, they should be punished according to their wickedness or the evil they have committed. Apparently God thinks quite differently.

Let the wicked forsake his way and the evil man his thoughts. Let him turn to the Lord, and He will have mercy on him, and to our God, for He will freely pardon. "For My thoughts are not your thoughts, neither are your ways My ways," declares the Lord. "As the heavens are higher than the earth, so are My ways higher than your ways and My thoughts than your thoughts" (Isaiah 55:7-9 NIV).

God is just, but the story just didn't seem like there was any justice involved. The only conclusion I had was that our thoughts are totally different in comparison to His thoughts. Unlike most humans, God seems to think from another angle. I couldn't buy into this story that God has a high tolerance for mortal sins and carnal folly. In most of the Bible, God doesn't seem to tolerate foolishness. So what was He looking for that would allow Him to move past the lying, conniving mistakes Jacob was making?

The only thing I could fathom was that Jacob, on some level, was *seeking God*. In the famous dream, "Jacob's Ladder" (see Gen. 28:12-16), Jacob dreams that God is talking to him and sees that this is God's place, and he honors God by using the stone he slept on for an altar. He vows to keep the Lord as his God and to tithe a tenth of his income to God (see Gen. 28:22). Now I did struggle with the "if/then" nature of his vow. *If*, God, You will take care of me, *then* I will tithe. But let's come back to that. Jacob was saying, "Tell me what to do and I am Yours." He was seeking God and honoring God, which are two very important things. Later on Jacob wrestles with an angel and, despite being injured, will not let go until he is blessed.

> *So Jacob was left alone, and a man wrestled with him till daybreak. When the man saw that he could not overpower him, he touched the socket of Jacob's hip so that his hip was wrenched as he wrestled with the man. Then the man said, "Let me go, for it is daybreak."*
>
> *But Jacob replied, "I will not let you go unless you bless me."*
>
> *The man asked him, "What is your name?"*
>
> *"Jacob," he answered.*
>
> *Then the man said, "Your name will no longer be Jacob, but Israel, because you have struggled with God and with men and have overcome"* (Genesis 32:24-28 NIV).

Jacob had his own fight with God, and they both won.

Symbolically or in real life, Jacob is holding onto God. Clearly this is Jacob's fight with God. He will not let go of God even when he is hurt. He demands that God bless him. Apparently angels on assignment have to return back to the Heavens by a certain time. This one could not stay past his permissible time or else he would get in trouble with God. It is not very clear why Jacob felt that this man could bless him. Somehow he knew that this man had a close connection with God. He probably felt that if he held this man hostage and asked for a ransom that God would grant it. This dogged determination often yields success in life. Even more so it seems the lesson is that this strong desire to be in connection with God has real advantages, even in the physical world we live in.

A reader might at first glance wonder how this wrestling differs from the resistance talked about in the last chapter. As mentioned earlier, resistance is putting up a wall or cutting off communication. That would have been walking away from God by not talking with Him or not listening to Him. In this event, Jacob is holding on and demanding a conversation, although it could easily be debated whether Jacob was listening.

Despite the excruciating pain that he must have suffered, Jacob continued to fight, exclaiming, "I will not let you go unless you bless me." How often in my struggles had I demanded God bless me? How often when I was hurting did I fight to stay connected to God, despite the seeming unfairness of the situation? Maybe at times, not enough. God not only blesses Jacob, He changes his name from "Jacob" to "Israel," a high honor. When God changes a person's name, it is accompanied by a change in that person's future and destiny. That's transformation. Jacob became Israel, out of which came the 12 tribes. How did a liar, a cheat, a thief, and a con become one of the most famous and celebrated people/nations in the entire Bible? It seems to be two things: (1) a relentless pursuit of God and (2) a demand to be blessed.

There are many good people in the Bible who never did any of those awful things, yet they did not make it on the "who's who" list in Scripture. I am beginning to believe that God really takes pleasure in fixing up people who are seriously damaged, causing them to have greater value than anyone could ever imagine. The King of transformation. This seeking of God is very important to not only us as humans but also Him. Apparently, if we are seeking God, He is willing to forgive some incredible mistakes.

> God really takes pleasure in fixing up people who are seriously damaged, causing them to have greater value than anyone could ever imagine.

IT ALL STARTED WITH MOTHER OR TIME

Have you ever been told that you act much like your mother or that you do things the same way that your father did? It makes sense. Whether it's DNA or learning to model ourselves after our parents, we seem to absorb much of their character. Since they are the first people we come in contact with, we quickly learn how they react to certain situations and begin to imitate them because we haven't learned our own personalities yet. Although this imitation helps us to learn about personalities and human characteristics in general, sometimes we can pick up bad emotional habits. Look at how Jacob seemed to model the conniving nature of his parents.

Rebekah was barren for 20 years before she gave birth to her twin sons, Jacob and Esau. Jacob was a momma's boy from the start. She favored him probably because Esau caused his parents much grief. Favoring Jacob meant that she wanted him to have a better life than Esau, and would go to extreme measures to make sure that happened. When Isaac became old, weakened in his flesh and nearly gone blind, he realized that it would probably be best to pass on the family's inheritance designated for his firstborn son Esau, as the culture during that time dictated.

Unlike inheritance in our modern-day society, this birthright was not only financial and material, it also included the passing on of a rich spiritual heritage. The birthright guaranteed future success. So it's pretty easy to accept why Jacob so badly coveted his brother's birthright. Knowing that Isaac was ready to pass on this special bequeathal, Rebekah raced to tell Jacob what she had heard and then concocted a plan to intercept the transfer.

> *"Prepare me the kind of tasty food I like and bring it to me to eat, so that I may give you my blessing before I die." Now Rebekah was listening as Isaac spoke to his son Esau. When Esau left for the open country to hunt game and bring it back, Rebekah said to her son Jacob, "Look, I overheard your father say to your brother Esau, 'Bring me some game and prepare me some tasty food to eat, so that I may give you my blessing in the presence of the Lord before I die.' Now, my son, listen carefully and do what I tell you: Go out to the flock and bring me two choice young goats, so I can prepare some tasty food for your father, just the way he likes it. Then take it to your father to eat, so that he may give you his blessing before he dies"* (Genesis 27:4-10 NIV).

Having only a short time to live, Isaac wanted to taste one of his favorite meals, specially prepared by his son. After that, he would give him the blessing. Rebekah could not wait to get back to Jacob to tell him what she discovered while eavesdropping. Obviously she shouldn't have been eavesdropping to begin with. Even if you happen to be around, it's not right to do that. There is supposed to be a special kind of bond between you and your spouse so that private information stays right with you and doesn't leak outside of that bond.

So if Rebekah was a loyal wife, whatever she heard her husband say would have stayed right there within her. Rebekah skillfully circumvented the entire process by running back to Jacob, informing him that he must go and kill two young goats and bring them back home immediately. Of course, Rebekah knew exactly how he would like his goat meat prepared, and she connived again. She prepared a meal for Isaac, deliberately misleading him into believing that it was made by his son.

Jacob said to Rebekah his mother, "But my brother Esau is a hairy man, and I'm a man with smooth skin. What if my father touches me? I would appear to be tricking him and would bring down a curse on myself rather than a blessing" (Genesis 27:11-12 NIV).

What a dishonest woman! Jacob wondered what might happen if his father asked to touch him, since he was smooth-skinned and his brother Esau was hairy like a beast in the field. How would he be able to actually convince his father that he was Esau and not Jacob, when his brother's features were so different than his? Rebekah skillfully made Jacob a master disguise from the goatskins. So we have it, Rebekah was full of deception; she had a con for everything. Whatever her motivation was for jeopardizing her own life, I am not sure. What I do know is that she was determined for Jacob to receive the birthright no matter what. Jacob conspired with her and was learning those traits of dishonesty.

Another lesson that jumped out at me from this was that you and I do not have to continue in the same negative behavioral patterns that our parents displayed. Just because a dad or mom didn't show affection, were not ambitious, lacked commitment in the marriage, or were alcoholics does not mean that you or I have to follow in those footsteps. You and I do have choices in life.

118

...you and I do not have to continue in the same negative behavioral patterns that our parents displayed.

One of the key choices is, are we going to doggedly pursue a connection to God and will we be relentless about demanding a great birthright as the son or daughter of a King? And when we mess up, will we choose to repent, forgive ourselves, and listen to what He wants us to do?

SELLING OUT FOR A BOWL OF STEW

Esau seemed to be the epitome of how not to react to a situation like this. People "sell out" for different reasons in life, but this one takes the cake. For 30 pieces of silver, Judas sold out Jesus. That's pretty bad, but at least silver has a trading value. Here, Esau sells his own birthright for a bowl of stew—simple peasant food, not even any kind of delicacy! How myopic or shortsighted can you be? That's something you just don't do. He gave in to the pressures of his hunger pains, having just returned from the big country, probably from hunting. This journey was quite a bit different than other journeys in that Esau's hunger was beyond the average. Yet he wasn't going to starve.

So a clear message here seemed to be, "Stay focused on the high importance of our birthright no matter our current circumstance." Don't sell out your future God-given dream because it's uncomfortable or scary. Don't settle for less than you deserve as one of God's kids, even if that means depriving the physical body. Don't take a relationship because it's convenient, when you know it's not the right person for you. Take a job that puts food on the table if you must, but keep looking for the opportunity to move into what you were born to do.

"Stay focused on the high importance of our birthright no matter our current circumstance."

And look at how Esau handled the deception, because that was another great lesson in what not to do. Yes, you'd think that your own family would care about your most crucial needs such as eating, having water, shelter, and clothing, and would meet those needs without question. One would expect a family member to be the first one to lend a helping hand. I thought to myself, *How could this rotten guy ever experience God's blessing in life?* So the "normal" reaction would be resentment, and that's what Esau did. However, that's not how Jacob handled deception by Laban. Jacob's response was to relentlessly pursue God; Esau just kept getting angry. Which solution seems to work? Repeatedly Esau is deceived and gets angry; and repeatedly when Jacob is deceived, he pursues God.

I May Be Old and Blind, But My Feelings Are Still Strong

Just because a person is blind doesn't mean that they are stupid. In fact, they may be more perceptive and intuitive than if they could see, having to rely on their inner strength and spiritual discernment. They begin to rely on their other senses. Isaac was definitely getting older, physically slower, and just breaking down. That is why he wanted to pass on the inheritance to his son before he died. When Jacob came before his blind father, his father noticed something strangely different about him. Jacob was able to fool him by making him believe that he was his hairy brother Esau.

When he came close to his father, his father sensed that the scent of Jacob smelled rather wilder than a human, more like an animal. That was definitely a characteristic of Esau. Personally, I tend to believe that his father really knew that it was he but just didn't have the strength to complain about it. People who are visually impaired tend to have an acute sense of awareness. They are very keen on things like smell, touch, and taste, having to rely much more on those things than sight. Faltering in his strength Isaac did not make an issue of the matter and proceeded to bestow his blessing on Jacob.

> *When Isaac caught the smell of his clothes, he blessed him and said, "Ah, the smell of my son is like the smell of a field that the Lord*

has blessed. May God give you of heaven's dew and of earth's richness—an abundance of grain and new wine. May nations serve you and peoples bow down to you. Be lord over your brothers, and may the sons of your mother bow down to you. May those who curse you be cursed and those who bless you be blessed" (Genesis 27:27-29 NIV).

Isaac heard Jacob's voice, but felt hairy hands and skin similar to Esau's on Jacob. Can you really fool someone who knows you? I'd know my dad's voice anywhere, and I am sure that he knows my voice also. After hearing a person's voice for many years, you automatically know who's speaking when you hear it without taking time to wonder. When God said to Adam in the garden, "Adam, where art thou," Adam didn't second-guess the voice of God thinking that he may have heard the voice of a ghost.

He knew that he was hearing God's voice and was confident that he was not hearing the voice of an imposter. Isaac could not only feel with his hands, but could also feel with the vibration of his inner witness, his spirit. Some things in life you don't have to contemplate; you just know. When he heard the voice of Jacob, I am sure that he knew what he was hearing, having heard the voice of Jacob since he was a small boy.

OK, you say, you really don't have any proof to validate your claim. Think about this, Jacob and Esau were twins, obviously fraternal. The most outward distinguishable mark is that one son was awfully hairy while the other one had smooth skin. That is a very major visible distinction; however, it is not the only distinction. Mothers and fathers know the voice of their child. I have three children, and if any one of them calls me on the phone, I never have to ask which one it is. To others, maybe my boys sound the same, but to me they sound different. I can always tell them apart by hearing their voices.

Automatically I know from the very first words who I am speaking to. Like Jacob, I can feel the vibration of their voice pattern and instantly know whom I am talking to. Isaac had this same experience. Strangely, he proceeded to confer the blessing upon an imposter rather than halt the ceremony and demand that the rightful inheritor come forth. Why he chose not to demand

MY FIGHT WITH GOD

more answers, or to even ask more probing questions, I do not know. It's the next journey of exploration of God's message for me.

A Short Recap

- Everything God does is right and all His ways are always just.

- God's thoughts are on a higher plane than yours.

- You are everything that God says you are.

- Your choices in life will determine the kind of outcome you will have.

- You may have inherited negative traits from your parents, but you don't have to keep them.

- Having a dogged determination may lead to great success in life.

- You will know the voice of the person whom you are intimately connected with.

- God loved risk-takers.

- Operating in *faith* always pleases God!

And without faith it is impossible to please God, because anyone who comes to Him must believe that He exists and that He rewards those who earnestly seek Him (Hebrews 11:6 NIV).

POINTS TO PONDER

1. How did Jacob, a liar, a cheat, a thief, and a con become one of the most famous and celebrated people/nations in the entire Bible? It seems to be because of two things. What are those two things?

_____

_____

_____

2. "You and I do not have to continue in the same negative behavioral patterns that our parents displayed." List some familial traits or behaviors that you would like to avoid. Now ask God to show you how to break these patterns and stop the cycle.

_____

_____

_____

3. Have you ever been tempted to settle for second-best? Do you ever lose sight of the birthright you have as a child of God? What can you do to stand firm in these situations?

_____

_____

_____

4. "You will know the voice of the person whom you are intimately connected with." Do you have trouble distinguishing the voice of God?

_____

_____

_____

5. *"Without faith it is impossible to please Him."* If you want to please God, don't you think it's important to learn what faith is and how you are supposed to exercise it?

_____

_____

_____

CHAPTER SEVEN

JESUS CURSES A HELPLESS TREE

The next day as they were leaving Bethany, Jesus was hungry. Seeing in the distance a fig tree in leaf, He went to find out if it had any fruit. When He reached it, He found nothing but leaves, because it was not the season for figs. Then He said to the tree, "May no one ever eat fruit from you again." And His disciples heard Him say it (Mark 11:12-14 NIV).

In the morning, as they went along, they saw the fig tree withered from the roots. Peter remembered and said to Jesus, "Rabbi, look! The fig tree You cursed has withered!" (Mark 11:20-21 NIV)

When I first read this, I thought, *What a petulant child this Jesus was!* He's hungry and wants figs, even though it's not the season. He wants what He wants when He wants it. So when there isn't any fruit there, He kills the tree. Doesn't that sound like a 4-year-old's temper tantrum to you? And He kills a helpless tree?! Earlier in Chapter Two we explored if God picked on rich people. Now I had to explore if He picked on helpless people. It sure didn't seem like the fig tree did anything wrong.

The outcome of being on the wrong side of God and Jesus was severe enough I almost didn't want to step into the ring with God on this one. However, an understanding of the difference between purpose and productivity and the importance of being clear on my purpose first has served me over and over again. There are several times in the 16-year history of Klemmer & Associates where this had led to a complete change of direction of the company. Our focus on the direct sale industry was a direct result of this lesson. This was also true of when I transitioned from being a speaking business centered on me to a business centered on our product, regardless of who the speaker or trainer was.

Is God a Production Fanatic?

Part of my problem was, why even bother cursing the tree? It wasn't as if this tree was no longer useful. The problem was that it was not performing the purpose for which Jesus had designated it *at the time* Jesus wanted it. Maybe His hunger had something to do with His reaction. Who knows? Perhaps Jesus thought that this tree missed a grand opportunity to actually feed a hungry Savior. I couldn't believe Jesus was acting like a 4-year-old throwing a tantrum. It just didn't fit everything else about Him and His story.

This Scripture troubled me until I started exploring the difference between purpose and productivity. The only one who decides true purpose is the creator of something. I could use a telephone as a paperweight, a weapon, or any number of things, but only the creator of the phone knows *why* they created it. The tree had many uses, but only God and Jesus through God would know the true purpose. My first thought would be that its purpose would be to produce figs, but I would be guessing unless I checked with God. Jesus must have checked with God and known its purpose was to feed Him, even though He knew it wasn't fig season.

Checking with God is the key to knowing our purpose. What a great revelation this was for me. How often was I checking in with God about what His purpose in a circumstance for me was? I must confess it was not very often at the time. I usually assumed I knew what the purpose was or if I didn't like the circumstance or experience then it had no purpose at all.

> **Checking with God is the key to knowing
> our purpose.**

So there seemed to be two sides to this. God was a production fanatic, but only within the context of His purpose. Miss either one of those and He was ruthless. We could be useful as a doctor or a teacher. That would be very productive. And yet we could be unfulfilled because it was not our God-given calling. In that case we did not know our purpose. There are many people who unhappily follow a career path for years and then decide they need to be doing something else. The fact is that they did not understand their true destiny and purpose from the beginning. Other people are happy with a career for years and then they realize it was a season; following their purpose, they move on to something else.

The point of this particular story is that we need to know the purpose God has for us and *then* be a production maniac. That's good stewardship. It's not our life or our invented purpose, but His. The whole idea behind producing really has to do with being more than average in an average world. Most Christians are average, and most of them tend to hate when anyone tries to provoke them to do more, be more, and have more in life.

> **...we need to know the purpose God has for us and
> *then* be a production maniac.**

Face it: being above average is really not difficult. You don't have to be Donald Trump, Warren Buffett, or Mary Lou Retton. Being above average simply means that you are effectively doing (bearing fruit) what *you* were created to do in life. When you do that, you automatically qualify as being above average.

Many people in the church fail to tap into their life's purpose. Without faith it is impossible to please God. God knows better than anyone else what brings pleasure to Him. Understand that acting in faith will raise the average person on all levels. Personally, I believe that God calls all believers to be above average. In fact, I actually believe that it's a sin to be average. You won't go to hell, because where you spend eternity is decided by your acknowledging God as your Lord and Savior. How you spend eternity there is a different story. For a great articulation of this, read John Bevere's *Driven by Eternity*. Now by "average" I do not mean compared to other people. By average I mean not doing the maximum you were called to do by God.

> **I actually believe that it's a sin to be average.**

Sin simply means that you missed the mark. You were close, but you didn't quite hit the target God expected. When you live an average lifestyle, you are really missing the mark of God. If you are created in the image and likeness of God, then how could you be average and feel good about it? Not everyone agrees with me on this point. I'm just voicing my heart, with the hope and expectation that someone may be blessed in the process, even if you don't come to the same conclusion. That's the value of a fight with God.

Pastor Larry Osborne, a great pastor and spiritual leader, strongly argues his point in one of my favorite books, *The Contrarian's Guide to Knowing God: Spirituality for the Rest of Us*:

> Could someone be average and still please God? What if God didn't want everyone to be turned into a leader and a hill-charging spiritual warrior? Could he possibly be pleased with simple folks who loved God, loved their family and friends, then died without ever doing (or wanting to do) anything outstandingly significant? The more I mulled this over, and the more closely I examined the Bible, the more convinced I became that the answer was yes. Mediocrity was actually an option—

and for some, a God pleasing option. It had to be. Because if it's impossible to be below average and please God, we have a BIG problem on our hands. Whatever we're measuring, and by whatever measure we use, half of us will always be on the wrong side of the average line, by the very definition of it.[1]

When I first read this, I thought, *Wow, here is a great guy willing to take the risk of writing a book voicing his "contrary thinking" toward how things have been traditionally taught and lived in the Church for centuries.* The very fact that he actually wrote such a controversial, against-the-grain book makes him an above-average Christian in my book. It's a great example of how wrestling with God deepens one's relationship and understanding *even* if they end up in a different conclusion. To do so as a pastor, a public figure, displays incredible courage.

I haven't had a conversation with Pastor Osborne although I want to in order to really get what he is driving at. For the moment I'm not so sure that mediocrity is even in God's vocabulary at all. It depends on whether mediocre is compared to other people or what God wants. Mediocrity, if it is less than what God wants for us, is something that many Christians have embraced in an attempt to hide from what they know they could be doing but are afraid to try. Lots of people refuse to do their best because of laziness, procrastination, dual focus, and just a lack of desire. *In my experience, many Christians are running away from their God-given calling just to avoid the possible disappointment of failure.*

> *...many Christians are running away from their God-given calling just to avoid the possible disappointment of failure.*

The challenge becomes a question of whose definition of mediocrity we are to use. Is it by the world's standard of what is important or by what God wants? So if God calls someone to be a great parent or to devote their time mentoring local children in youth sports, then do not judge them for not making a lot of money or not having a powerful position. However, if God called someone to be a parent and mentor local youth in sports and they ignored this obligation, then I would say God might be ruthless like He was with the tree.

Without question, God loves everybody. Anyone who confesses with their mouth that Jesus is Lord and believes in their heart that God raised Him from the dead will definitely go to Heaven. However, just because God loves you and you love God does not mean that you are pleasing to Him. I love all of my children. There have been times when they may have done things or said things that I was displeased with. I didn't throw them away or cast them out, yet they knew that I was displeased. So it brings pleasure to God when you produce the way that you were designed to.

The point here is not to make someone feel like less of a person just because they don't produce like someone else. That leads to materialism, competitiveness, and greed. That road is lonely and unfulfilling. You should not feel bad if you can't produce books and beautiful poetry, especially if you are not a writer. God only measures your ability to produce in relation to your purpose. Production in terms of our life experiences cannot always be measured in terms of quantity. The "more and more" mind-set is really a futile one, in that you never seem to find the satisfaction you are looking for.

Once you get more, something inside of you says, "That's not enough." And then you start out on a long journey trying to find fulfillment by acquiring more stuff. Genuine fulfillment can only come through knowing your purpose and who you are in God. God is definitely concerned with quality. What kind of fruit can you give God from your life? Can you give God a quality life that mirrors the very image of His excellence? Or is your life lacking substance?

Although at first I really didn't understand why Jesus cursed the fig tree, since I saw many other necessary functions for it, at least now I somewhat understood. Most people in society can do various things and often they do them well. The question is, are they doing what they were called to do? What matters most to God is when you do exactly what He created you to do. For example, if God called you to stand in the middle of the San Francisco-Oakland Bay Bridge for an entire month, and do nothing else except to just stand there, then in doing so you would be fulfilling your purpose in life.

People in society would consider you weird and perhaps judge you as being "less than." I believe God would rejoice in your obedience and productiveness. Most people would be too concerned about what other people may think of them to take such a step of obedience. That is usually why people stay average. People tend to need other people's permission to succeed, when really all they need is God's approval. Everybody's calling is uniquely different. So it doesn't make sense to compare your call to another person's calling. Everybody is called to do something. Whether or not that thing is super-spectacular in the eyes of humans is unimportant.

It reminds me of my friend Jim Stovall. As I mentioned in an earlier chapter, he won a gold medal at the Olympics, received the Humanitarian of the Year award (along with Mother Teresa), owns a satellite television network, produced and owns a Hollywood movie starring Brian Denehy and James Garner, has written best-selling books, and boasts many other achievements. The unique thing is that he often says that the most influential person in his life was a mentally challenged young boy named Christopher who died at the age of six. His biggest achievement in the world was that he finally learned to climb stairs and tie his shoes before he died. But Christopher was blind, and when Jim Stovall went blind in his twenties, Christopher inspired Jim to be all that Jim is today. Through Jim telling his story, Christopher has inspired millions. God has His own purpose.

The bottom line is that we need to do what God calls us to do. God will measure us by our willingness and desire to fulfill His purpose. The fig tree failed to do what God created it to do, thus bringing a curse upon itself.

There are many books written about discovering your purpose, such as Rick Warren's immensely popular *The Purpose Driven Life*. Since purpose comes from God, the first thing to do is to get alone with God and pray and ask what your purpose is. In my own life there are certain signposts that helped me identify my purpose. Identify what skills you are naturally good at, what might be called your gifts. It may be a talent like music, public speaking, math, or something like being friendly or organized. Write your top two or three down instead of a whole laundry list. It's hard, but limit it to the top three. Now write down your top values. These are things you hold to be so important you will abide by this value even when no one is looking or knows you are following. This might be honesty, having a team approach, caring for others, or pursuit of excellence. Again, avoid the tendency to make a long list and limit yourself to the top three. Both your gifts and core values are like sign posts that are pointing you toward your purpose and what I believe God is calling you to do. In my experience, purpose is always in one way or another about other people. It is an overarching "why" statement behind everything you do. It is like direction and never-ending. Unlike an objective, you never get there, but you are on the path or off the path. You may now find it helpful to talk with someone about a strategy or mechanism to best identify objectives and whether your career is directly in the field of your purpose or whether your purpose is supporting what you do as a career. For example, let's say you discover your purpose is to share God's love with as many people as possible. You could have a career as a church staff member and it is directly in that field. Then again, you could be a street sweeper and it is the motive and way you do that job.

How Not To Whist Away

If the tree failed to produce fruit, it eventually would have withered away. That was a message right there for me. How many people do you know who have retirement as a goal? Now retirement is many things to many people. For most, it means not working and living a life of leisure. I am not so sure that type of retirement is biblical. However, I am not saying that you have to pound nails as a carpenter for 10 hours a day until you die of a heart attack. I am simply questioning if being nonproductive is a worthy goal. It would seem, based on this story, that the goal is always: How do I pursue my purpose? That might look very different at 75 than at age 45 or age 25. If we begin measuring productiveness in terms of our purpose, then we would be constantly looking for new vehicles or means to fulfill that purpose. How does one provide fruit or fulfill one's purpose while they are trying to pay the bills? Not making this your first priority and looking for ways to fulfill their purpose gives more options.

Many times I have heard of stories where a senior citizen had worked diligently for 30 or 40 years and then retired. Within one year of retiring their health began to decline and then they died. Another scenario is a couple, married for 50+ years, one spouse dies and then shortly after the other one follows. Why does this happen to so many people in life? Is it because people got lost in what they were doing and forgot their purpose? Even when one is young and goal-driven, if they forget *why* they are going after a goal they'll eventually burn out.

When you freely give of yourself, sowing your time, money, resources, and wisdom into others, you are alive and energetic, and you create an atmosphere that prolongs your own life. A friend of mine, Pastor Stenneth Powell, a pastor in Raleigh, North Carolina, has a vision to build a first-class state-of-the-art residential complex for senior citizens within his church and community. This housing facility, run by a foundation in connection with his Abundant Life Church, will pay for all of the senior citizens' expenses.

The only requirement from the seniors is that they share their personal lifelong experiences with a child at least three times weekly to create a lasting bond. It has been documented that these kinds of healthy relationships between the young and the older people causes the more matured adults to discover a new lease on life, extending their years far beyond the average expectation.

I've seen young adults and even teenagers who choose to give up, lose heart, and just quit on life. At a young age they begin to dry up. The cure: Always be in pursuit of your purpose. Always know that someone needs you. Always recognize that you are full of purpose and potential. The fig tree that Jesus cursed may have still existed today, if it only knew that Jesus needed a fig for His sustenance. The tree had a greater purpose but did not realize it. Remember that your potential is not about you but rather the people whom you are called to help live. Bear fruit!

> **Always recognize that you are full of purpose and potential.**

MY FIGHT WITH GOD

But now we move to the next problem. If this tree continued to not produce figs, then in all fairness the tree would have dried up anyway. Why did Jesus make a special point of cursing it and having it immediately wither and die? That's pretty dramatic. The disciples are amazed the next day to see it dead. Jesus then delivers what seems to be the two messages or points He wanted to make:

> *"Whatever things you ask when you pray, believe that you receive them, and you will have them....If you have anything against anyone, forgive him, that your Father in heaven may also forgive you..."* (Mark 11:24-25).

Sending a Strong Message About Forgiveness

Let me address forgiveness, although it may seem irrelevant. A tree doesn't have fruit; Jesus kills it. How did forgiveness tie in? I wasn't sure how a tree would forgive, but it seemed Jesus was saying, "Don't mess with Me." Also, forgiveness is a major issue that you do not want to fool around with or you will suffer most dire consequences.

For me, an appropriate amount of fear is a good thing. A constant state of fear is a "spirit of fear," which the Bible says to avoid. But fear is still a valuable thing. This analogy has certainly caused me to think after someone has really done me wrong and asked me to forgive them, even when I didn't feel like it. If you are afraid of the consequences of having a flat tire with no spare, you carry a spare. You have fear, but not a spirit of fear. (Later on I would figure out how resentment interferes in me being with God, in the flow of God and enjoying the abundance He wants me to have.)

It's Always Your Season

It bugged me that it says it wasn't the season for figs, and yet Jesus still expected figs. Did Jesus expect fruit *all* the time? Something didn't seem right. One of the great things about a fight with God today is that you can look at and compare how different scholars in the past have interpreted pieces of Scripture through commentaries and you can look at how different Bibles even print a line of Scripture. For example, I had read one commentary using the Amplified Bible, which has, in quotes, saying it was the season. Yet in Old King James, New King James, New International Version, New Living Translation, New American Standard Bible, and every other Bible I could find, it clearly stated it was not the season. Then I read *The Bible Knowledge Commentary*, which said that the Palestinian fig trees produce small edible buds in March, followed by the appearance of large green leaves in early April, followed by the full figs. The small edible buds were sometimes eaten by the common people. It was simply different fruit in a different season.

When I was young I didn't really understand or care about "potential." Pretty much I did what I knew that I could do and just kept moving forward. While others made a big deal of doing their best, I just assumed that what I was doing was the best I could do. I came into the understanding of potential after I was exposed to teachings about it and understood more about the Bible.

When you really think about it, nearly all of the stories in the Bible deal with man's potential in God. The failures of great men and women in the Bible can only be viewed as failure because they didn't reach their highest potential. Everybody fails. Failure is not the worst thing in the world. Giving up is. People usually give up when they no longer believe that they have the potential to do what they were created to do. That's what happens when people lose sight of intention. God places purposeful intention within all of His creations. The only one who can abort intention is you.

> **Failure is not the worst thing in the world.
> Giving up is.**

The acorn has within it the God-given power of intention to become an oak tree. It realizes its potential. It doesn't have to try hard or labor long hours to become—it just does. The caterpillar does not strive to become a butterfly.

The power of God-given intention lives inside the caterpillar, and without struggle it becomes a beautiful butterfly. In this parable, the fig tree had the potential to bear fruit, yet contradicted its purpose. When you contradict your God-given purpose, you will live in continual conflict. Maybe that is the reason why so many people in the world struggle from day to day to find joy and happiness.

> **When you contradict your God-given purpose, you will live in continual conflict.**

I don't know whether some people's lives were designed to be a struggle and others an enjoyable process. I do know there is a different experience around circumstances most people call happiness versus the deep enjoyment that comes when you are playing full out in pursuit of one's God given purpose. People confuse the two feelings. Paul was chained to a soldier's leg and still felt joy because he was in alignment with his purpose. He was not happy in the circumstance, which is fleeting based on the circumstance, but he was content.

Before I was saved, I did not have a bad life at all. I grew up in a suburban, middle-class neighborhood in New Jersey. My parents were far from poor, and I had all of the things that I needed in life. Looking back, I'm sure that I could have survived until now if I continued to live my life at that humdrum level. But the question is, would I be content or joyful? I would not because it didn't align with my purpose. Honestly, I wouldn't be joyful not knowing God although I could be happy in the momentary circumstance.

My spiritual desire to even read the Bible was definitely connected to a yearning within my soul to live a fuller life. Like the fig tree, I had a whole lot of leaves, but I didn't have any fruit. I was not living up to my fullest potential. In fact, I would not be able to impact the thousands of lives that I do today, if I were not maximizing my potential. The fig tree could not do anything to satisfy Jesus' hunger because it was not considering the God-giving potential already built in.

Pastor Larry Osborne takes a different position here again, writing a chapter in his book entitled: *The Potential Trap: Why Being All We Can Be Might Be a Dumb Idea*. He writes:

> For years the United States military poured millions of dollars into a recruiting campaign built around the simple statement, "Be all that you can be." It proved to be an incredibly powerful marketing slogan, resonating with the conventional wisdom of our age, a wisdom that proclaims maximizing our potential as one of life's sacred responsibilities. I find most Christians drink from the same cup. We tend to see unfulfilled potential as a tragic shame; squandered opportunity as a sinful choice. We assume that God couldn't possibly be pleased with anyone who settles for being less than the best they can be—in any area of life. But it's a lie. Potential is not a sacred responsibility. Potential is a harsh mistress—seductive, never satisfied, prone to exaggeration, nearly impossible to figure out. Those who pursue her inevitably end up in the poisoned land of self-centered priorities and me-first decisions.[2]

Because some of his views differ from mine, you might think I didn't like Pastor Osborne's book; actually, I loved it. It caused me to think as I hope this book does with you. Some conclusions he has are the same as mine and others are different. In this case I don't believe it is either-or. In my book, *The Compassionate Samurai*, I separate the domains of "satisfaction" and a different domain called "more-better-different." In the arena of more-better-different there can always be more, so what Pastor Larry is saying would be true. That is the arena of happiness based on circumstance, which is fleeting. In the arena of satisfaction I can always be satisfied or content if I am in alignment with my purpose. Have you ever noticed that when you are in alignment with your purpose you have a certain feeling of contentment, regardless if circumstances are difficult? This is why Paul can be chained to a soldier's leg and be content. Problems occur when we confuse these two feelings of contentment and "happiness" or how we try and get the particular feeling. We can play both games, but should not confuse the two experiences.

I am only bringing his work into this conversation because this guy reminds me of myself. He is daring enough to take on totally unconventional arguments. More than that, I realize that what he is saying through his writing really echoes the voice of many Christians and seekers who aren't brave enough to say it. Maybe the ways the Church has presented the whole idea about potential have scared people away from embracing it. The brand of potential that the Church seeks after may be somewhat unclear, confusing, or unrealistic all together.

My mentor helped me to discover things about myself that I would have never dreamt. The potential was there. I just had to realize it. The cursed fig tree stood there, helpless, attracting sympathy from the disciples because it failed to realize its potential. When people feel sorry for you, it's usually because you are not projecting a sense of confidence. The onlooker looks at you, sees a curse, and will continue to see you that way until you become the person that God intended you to be.

Interestingly enough, Jesus' disciples never recognized their fullest potential as long as Jesus was alive. In some ways, they lived their lives allowing Jesus to do everything for them. After Jesus died, that is when many of the disciples rose to the occasion and began to "walk on water." I can relate all too well. As long as my mentor, Tom, was leading his seminars and conducting personal training throughout the United States, I was right there to help him. But after he died, it took me a little while to do what I had learned.

> **Jesus' disciples never recognized their fullest potential as long as Jesus was alive.**

Like the fig tree, I didn't immediately realize my potential either. It was in me, but I was the one who had to acknowledge it and begin the process of walking in that reality. So there is no need to make excuses for why some people do not tap into their potential. It doesn't help making them believe that it's all right to do nothing in life. Doing nothing is a royal waste of God's time and also yours. God made everybody in the universe with a specific assignment.

And I believe that it is a pastor's job and a mentor's place to help draw that assignment out of you.

A Short Recap

- Do exactly what God created you to do. That matters most.

- You are only expected to produce in life that which God created you to produce, nothing more.

- Genuine fulfillment can only come through knowing who you are in God.

- The goal is not in bearing the most fruit, but rather bearing the right fruit.

- Failure is not the worst thing in the world; giving up is.

- When you contradict your God-given purpose, you will live in constant conflict.

- Your potential is not about you but rather the people whom you are called to help live.

- Regardless of how old you are, you never stop bearing fruit!

POINTS TO PONDER

1. What did you think of the story of Jesus cursing the fig tree in Mark 11 the first time you read it?

_____

_____

_____

2. "Checking with God is the key to knowing our purpose." Have you checked with God lately? Have you asked Him specifically what your purpose is?

_____

_____

_____

3. "Many Christians are running away from their God-given calling just to avoid the possible disappointment of failure." Do you live your life in fear of failure? Do you ignore God's plans for your life because you are afraid you don't have what it takes to succeed? Ask yourself this: What would I do differently in my life if it was impossible for me to fail?

_____

_____

_____

4. If you are doing what God wants you to do and are in His will, is it even possible for you to be a failure?

_____

_____

_____

ENDNOTES

1. Larry Osbourne, *The Contrarian's Guide to Knowing God: Spirituality for the Rest of Us* (Multnomah Books, 2007), 45.

2. Larry Osbourne, *The Potential Trap: Why Being All We Can Be Might Be a Dumb Idea* (The Doubleday Religious Publishing Group, April 2007), 187.

CHAPTER EIGHT

WHAT'S UP WITH THE BE-ATTITUDES?

Blessed are the poor in spirit, for theirs is the kingdom of heaven.

Blessed are those who mourn, for they will be comforted.

Blessed are the meek, for they will inherit the earth.

Blessed are those who hunger and thirst for righteousness, for they will be filled.

Blessed are the merciful, for they will be shown mercy.

Blessed are the pure in heart, for they will see God.

Blessed are the peacemakers, for they will be called sons of God.

Blessed are those who are persecuted because of righteousness, for theirs is the kingdom of heaven.

Blessed are you when people insult you, persecute you and falsely say all kinds of evil against you because of Me. Rejoice and be glad, because great is your reward in heaven, for in the same way they persecuted the prophets who were before you (Matthew 5:3-12 NIV).

Just like all of the other sections I selected, these attitudes just didn't seem to make much sense. First the passage seemed to be telling me that I didn't need to be passionate or aggressive, but instead I could just sit around and cry or feel bad for myself to get into Heaven. Then it says to be a weakling and you will get everything. Then be merciful and that's how your enemies will be to you. And while you are at it, just rejoice that you are being persecuted because you will be rewarded later. What planet was the writer of this Scripture living on? It sure didn't seem relevant in the world where I lived.

And yet my struggles with this Scripture proved it to be crucially relevant. The insights around inheriting the earth through meekness has helped me overcome challenges like having one of my trainers betray me and then try and steal the business from me. The notion of being poor in spirit as being better than confidence has allowed me to attract other powerful people to be on our company's mission. In a way you could say it has become a foundation for having the right attitude.

We already know how I feel about ideas being pushed on me, right? Luckily I've become more at peace with the fact that I won't always see God's viewpoint at first and hopefully by now you've seen how fighting with God can be productive!

Not only were the "attitudes" confusing, but back then I didn't like being told how to be. I felt that I was my own man. I did what I wanted to do and I didn't feel that I needed anybody's advice on how I should or should not be. It was the same idea as my thoughts on resistance. My thoughts were, "Nobody tells me what to do or how to be. People who need others to tell them what to do are weak. If they can't make a decision on their own, then that's pretty pathetic." To me, there wasn't anything wrong with the way that I was.

My first take on these "attitudes" was that maybe the situation of their specific culture and region made the ideas relevant and easy to achieve. If that were the case, then all right. I could cope with that reality. But when you try to bring these attitudes and character traits into the 20th and 21st centuries, they need to work and be relevant. They had to make some kind of sense. I wanted to see an example of someone successfully doing the things that Jesus said to do in the modern business world, or one of my peers living by these lessons. If I couldn't find anybody (and I was pretty sure I wouldn't), then I would pretty much forget about it.

Blessed Are the Meek

Blessed are the meek, for they will inherit the earth (Matthew 5:5).

It seemed like the Bible was telling me to just lie down and allow people to walk all over me, like that kid who always got beat up in school. If I stayed on the ground and allowed them to do that, then I was being meek. I wanted no part of that. If "meek" meant that I had to be taken advantage of, then no thank you. Yet the Bible was not only saying to be meek, it also said that if I was, I would inherit the whole earth. That got my attention. Here was a way to get all the goodies. But having to be meek just brought me to a halt.

Now the man Moses was very meek, above all the men which were upon the face of the earth (Numbers 12:3 KJV).

Now this is a guy who choked a builder to death with his bare hands! Murder doesn't sound meek to me. I tried to write off that incident as his straying from the path, but then Moses led two million people on a march. In my military days, I had an infantry company of 100+ men, and then I was a logistics officer for about 700 men. Even under my own company, I am the leader for 50 people. I know what it's like to get just these small groups going in one direction. It's *not easy!* I couldn't believe Moses was meek and led two million people.

Recently, I have come to the realization (mostly through my kids) that my definitions of certain words are old-fashioned. Words like "cool" and "phat" bring to mind entirely different meanings to me when *I* hear them versus when my kids or a younger generation do. Words change over time, and while their new meanings may not make much sense to you, it's better to accept this transition and move on. It struck me that this understanding might be helpful in tackling yet another lesson from God.

So I had to come to grips with the fact that I had to expand my own knowledge of word meanings to really understand the Bible more clearly. The Bible was translated into English around 1610. If the words "fat" or "cool" could change meanings over 15 years, could the word "meek" change over 400 years? If you look at a French Bible in that time period, they more accurately translate it as "gentlemanly." I thought of "gentlemanly" as putting other people first, much like a guy opening the car door for a woman. That made a little more sense, but I still wasn't totally getting it. Then I found out that the Greek word for meek meant "submissive."

Now there is a word that throws some people into a tizzy. *Submissive*, according to *Webster's New World Dictionary*, means "to yield to the control or power of another."¹ Well, what was Moses submissive to? We could see he certainly was *not* submissive, especially in Exodus 17, to the whines and groans of the people as they complained on the journey and kept telling him they wished they were back in Egypt. The important thing was that *Moses was submissive to the will of God*. Well, most of the time. That's what gave him all his power! Look what happened to him the one time he wasn't submissive. God yanked the prize out from him and didn't let him go to the Promised Land. So maybe there is something to being submissive to the will of God and getting all the goodies.

But then my problems started. First of all, how did God talk to you? Was it a voice? That seemed to be how Moses did it. But me, I didn't hear any voices. It seemed to be just a feeling. But that created another problem. Was this "feeling" from my subconscious or God? If the "feeling" came from God, it had to be correct because He is infinite, but that wasn't necessarily true if the feeling came from my subconscious mind or heart. For example, suppose I had a feeling not to go down a dark alley. If it was from God, He knows all, so there really is a dangerous person down that alley. If it was from my subconscious or heart, it could simply be a fear of the dark and there is no actual danger down the alley. So I had to start practicing through trial and error to distinguish which feeling came from where.

Then there was the whole challenge of simply taking time to listen to God. Sometimes I would just get so busy trying to control my life that I would forget to stop and simply listen to see if He was trying to tell me something. That still can be a challenge. And then of course there was the problem of actually submitting to what I thought God was trying to tell me. Moses was meek because he both clearly heard God and he was submissive to the will of God. In other words he submitted his number one or conscious mind to the third level, God, and allowed Him to make the decisions.

> **Moses was meek because he both clearly heard God and he was submissive to the will of God.**

Most people run their whole lives with the conscious mind, which includes the five physical senses, reason, and logic. In fact, many people pride themselves on being reasonable. This then becomes the box they live inside of. Making the choice to submit your conscious mind to God does not mean you throw reason and logic out the window. It means reason and logic become a tool, not the master. This is what being in alignment with God is all about. When the conscious mind, subconscious mind, and God are all lined up, *then* you attract all of the goodies in life like a magnet. The difficult parts are hearing the word of God, submitting the conscious mind to God, and getting the subconscious to agree.

Getting the subconscious mind to agree is no easy task either. One's subconscious mind can be out of alignment or clogged so that God cannot flow through you. Many Christians know how to tithe in their conscious mind. They can quote Scripture such as Malachi 3:10 about the promises of tithing. However, if the subconscious has a scarcity belief that there is not enough or it believes that when you give away you will have less, then it discourages the conscious mind from taking action and you will not tithe. This is one reason why historically only 7 percent of declared Christians in the U.S. tithe. You have to align or submit your subconscious mind with God as well as submit your conscious mind to God. In changing the beliefs of our subconscious there

are three methods I am aware of. One is prayer and God's direct interven-
tion. Another is repetition of a behavior. The third is an emotional experience.
Some speakers say that you can change a habit or mind-set in 21 days with a
repeated behavior change. That is not my experience. I have had some habits
and mind-sets that have changed instantly and others that took years. The
difference seems to be how much emotion is involved and that is why in the
Klemmer & Associates trainings we have so many games or experiences. The
more emotion, the less repetition is needed. When a person first starts tithing, they may have a contrary belief much like I did that giving away means
having less (like giving a piece of cake away and there is less cake left on the
table). Because I was emotional around money, this was a repetitive (every time
I got paid) and emotional behavior. Over time my belief system shifted where
I saw that some games were fixed in quantity like the cake and other games
like money and love were not. That is an example of bringing the conscious,
subconscious, and God all lined up.

BLESSED ARE THE POOR IN SPIRIT

Blessed are the poor in spirit, for theirs is the kingdom of heaven
(Matthew 5:3).

Even religious scholars like to debate the meaning of this particular beatitude. One group believes that the poor in spirit are literally people with no
money. I think some of the confusion stems from one of my earlier points:
what exactly does "poor" mean to us? Most people automatically assume that
it means lack of money. I, however, did not subscribe to that meaning because
of the word "spirit." That had nothing to do with money for me. My problem
with this Scripture was that being "poor in spirit" to me meant either poor in a
spiritual spirit *or* that I had no fighting spirit, desire, or will to do something.
I couldn't see how either of those viewpoints pleased God.

Now I have come to see this use of the phrase "poor in spirit" as really another way of restating humility. Humility comes from a slightly different angle
than being submissive and obedient to God. This comes from having an open
mind, spiritually speaking. The head, or first part of our snowman (or snow

woman if you like), must be willing to admit that it doesn't and can't know everything. It requires for us to have an inquiring beginner's mind. People who believe they know everything about the Bible or God are not going to be blessed because they do not have a humble attitude. Once we think we know everything, there is no space for God or new knowledge. The poor in spirit always realize that God is bigger than the limited revelation they have of Him.

> **Once we think we know everything, there is no space for God or new knowledge.**

By being open to God, not only are you showing that you have a beginner's mind-set, you are also showing that you are empty and need to be refilled. When you live life before God, recognizing that you always need to be filled and then re-filled again and again, you are the poor in spirit. You are open to God. This will be the kind of person who is going to be blessed! There is no shame in allowing room for learning and growth within you. This does not demean the knowledge that you hold already but readies you to grow mentally and spiritually through God.

An opposite of "poor in spirit" is a person full of "churchy" pride who thinks that they have a revelation of the Bible and that this revelation makes them better than people who don't see it the same way. It violates the commandment to love others as ourselves. For example, when people judge my spirituality based on my business decisions, I question their ways of thinking. Once there was a certain Christian businessman who didn't believe I was a mature Christian, based on one of my decisions. There was nothing unethical or immoral in the decision. It simply wasn't the decision he would have made. Disagreeing with my business decision is fine and I welcome that feedback. But to extrapolate that means I am poor and my spirituality is faulty? And would his attitude make me more or less desirous of following Christ?

The opposite of being poor in spirit is being judgmental, which isolates us from the very people we care about and are called to help. The businessman who questioned my spirituality based on what he saw as the wrong business decision didn't even consider that I might be able to minister to a totally different audience and introduce them to Christ in the process because of the decision I made. He also disrespected me by automatically ignoring me once he found out about this decision. What image of "Christianity" did that give people watching his behavior? He couldn't consider or see any of that until being "poor in spirit." That's what I mean by not having openness to spiritual things and thinking that you know everything. That's dangerous and it really doesn't represent God at all.

> The opposite of being poor in spirit is being judgmental...

BLESSED ARE THOSE WHO MOURN

Blessed are those who mourn, for they will be comforted (Matthew 5:4).

When I first read this, I thought of mourners like a bunch of whining cry-babies. My home life and my military training had told me to simply "tough it out." I never really allowed myself to need anybody's comfort. I looked at comfort as a pat on the back. What were the benefits in mourning and being comforted? There weren't many clear to me. Ask a vegetarian what the benefits are in eating filet mignon and what do you think they'd say? No benefit. I'm not saying that people don't need comfort in life. What I am saying is that when I was in my twenties, I didn't see I needed it.

All my life, I had parents who loved me. They never hit me. They believed I could do anything. In many ways, I had an ideal childhood. Since I hadn't really seen life in all of its many variations, I did not need comfort because I hadn't gone through anything all that bad. I guess that comfort is only a thing you desire when you've gone through a traumatic situation. If not, you probably don't need it. That's how I thought, and so this piece of Scripture was a non-issue.

Blessed Are Those Who Hunger and Thirst for Righteousness

Blessed are those who hunger and thirst for righteousness, for they shall be filled (Matthew 5:6).

This one seemed to be the least of my problems. Righteousness in my opinion was, "I am right; you are wrong." I did not see it as being right with God's viewpoint.

And what were these people going to be filled with? Maybe filled with their own self-importance, but I didn't see why they would be blessed or Jesus would be promoting it. As you can see from this book, God did create a hunger in me for His viewpoint. To me, we don't get to see God's viewpoint many times unless we have that hunger or burning desire to find out. Hence having a fight with God can be a good thing.

Blessed Are the Merciful

Blessed are the merciful, for they shall obtain mercy (Matthew 5:7).

Who cares about mercy? Earlier, in my twenties, I looked at mercy as pity or special treatment and I didn't want either. Part of this came from my framework from sports. I played football in high school and was only 5'7" and 170 pounds, but I didn't want any mercy or special treatment. In fact, I reveled in the challenge. I made up for my size in hustle and toughness. In academics, it was the same. I certainly was not the smartest kid around, but I would study more than other people. "Give me a shot" was all I asked.

At West Point, I did great at law studies. Later on, I became convinced that law had nothing to do with justice. I saw law as little to do with justice and everything to do with who could argue the case better. I was interested only in justice—giving people what they deserve. An eye for an eye kind of thing. That was what seemed fair. So here is a key distinction.

Justice is giving people what they deserve.

Mercy is not giving people what they deserve.

Grace is giving people more than they deserve.

Prior to being a Christian, I was totally into justice and saw little benefit in mercy. Grace wasn't even on my radar.

The other problem I had with this beatitude is that even if I gave mercy, it didn't mean others would reciprocate like the Scripture implied. That wasn't how things worked in my world. Mean people were mean, period. Sometimes the person to whom you show the most mercy may end up stabbing you in the back. Was he asking us to be merciful to an Adolf Hitler or a Saddam Hussein?

An interesting and more recent historical parallel is when the Jews retook Jerusalem in the Six-Day War, and they allowed the Muslims to keep the holy citadel as a sign of mercy. When I talked to Muslims while visiting the country, they told me they saw this gesture as a sign of weakness. It is interesting to note though, if you study the history during the Crusades, the great Muslim warrior Saladin was revered even by Christians for being "merciful." Although fierce in battle, in sieges of cities he would repeatedly let people leave safely if they surrendered the city. Also, look at the whole "reconciliation" movement after apartheid in Africa—the victims gave amnesty to their perpetrators if they publicly confessed and repented. It was believed that the victim could not heal without the attacker healing as well, because we are all connected.

And perhaps the mercy you receive back would come from someone other than to whom it was given. That's how it has seemed to work in my life. After being taken advantage of in a lawsuit, I recovered all the money and much more through people, strategies, and opportunities that I can't even begin to explain. If we are all connected, then it is all coming back through God anyway. The more I saw the connectedness of humanity, the more "Kingdom" principles made sense. But when I started my Christian walk I had no interest in receiving mercy, couldn't see any benefits in it, and I didn't believe it was ever truly reciprocated.

Suppose the game was rigged?! This really made it interesting. Suppose in the arena of academics I studied hard, scored well, and then they gave the better grade to someone else? Suppose I stopped someone short of what they needed for a first down in football and the referee decided to give it to them anyway? If the game is rigged, it is out of your control no matter what.

Have you ever wanted something that you could not have? The most fascinating thing with Heaven to me was that I couldn't earn my way in. That was so contrary to the way I thought the world worked. No amount of hustle would do it. No matter how many good things I did it wouldn't get me in. That astounded me. If I wanted eternity in Heaven, then I needed mercy and grace.

The amazing part was that God was showing me mercy whether I accepted it or not. Jesus gave His life for me, and I didn't do anything to deserve that. That's grace. To acknowledge that fact was a huge ego buster for me. I felt very vulnerable. What helped was that I saw God opened Himself up to unbelievable rejection by giving up His son and people could still say no. He shows mercy to us and encourages us to do the same.

However, the way that God shows mercy may be different than you or I expect. God shows mercy through the simple things that we often overlook. Maybe God showed me mercy by introducing me to my mentor Tom Willhite. Not everyone gets the privilege to be mentored like I was. I didn't do anything special to deserve that. Yes, I did my part in solving problems for him and earning time with him. But there were also things like living in a city where he did classes regularly and having a friend who had been to his seminars introduce me to him. That was God's grace.

I, and you, if you haven't already, must choose to be saved. That's our end of responsibility. But it's a fixed game in that it was His blood that forgave all our sins. God giving His son's life for me is grace because I certainly didn't deserve it. Perhaps grace trumps justice, although justice is still necessary. They both are important and have their place. Mercy determines where we spend eternity and justice determines how we spend eternity. (Again I recommend reading John Bevere's excellent book, *Driven by Eternity.*) The motivation for me has been to look for places where I need to show mercy and grace instead of simply justice.

Mercy determines where we spend eternity and justice determines how we spend eternity.

Often I use money to illustrate grace, and using it to illustrate grace is much easier than just being kind and caring. In running our company, I try to have justice in how people are paid. They are paid in proportion to their adding value to the marketplace. At the same time, there are places where grace is shown and money is given, not based on how much work they've done. There are also times where mercy is shown when a mistake is made and is not punished or punished to the level it calls for. My mentor always urged us to give money to charity. He knew that by doing this, we were exercising not only generosity but also grace. Now, in my own business, I encourage our graduates to spend as much time donating to and working for charities as possible.

BLESSED ARE THE PURE IN HEART

Blessed are the pure in heart, for they shall see God (Matthew 5:8).

Why suggest something that no one can live up to? "Pure" seems unrealistic and unattainable, like finding water in a desert. I didn't know anybody who was really pure in heart. Of course, I was looking at their purity from my myopic viewpoint, not God's. I've always held leaders to a higher standard than everyone else. I expect people to lie, but I don't exactly expect a president to lie. So when the President does, I think, *Hey, if the President is lying, cheating, and stealing and he holds the highest office, then who in the nation is really pure in heart?*

Today, I look at the pure in heart as those who are *in pursuit of excellence* or perfection. Purity or perfection is not a destination as much as a process. The pursuit of purity is like driving a car toward a destination. Although we may not reach the destination of perfect purity until we get to Heaven, our job is to know where we are headed and to make constant steering adjustments in order to keep the car on the right road to our destination. It's the pursuit of a pure heart that keeps you on the path. Those doing so will definitely be blessed, even if they sway from one side to the other. So the key is in working at it.

> **Purity or perfection is not a destination as much as a process.**

With a "pure" heart or subconscious mind, and in the context of our snow-man analogy, we have an open pipeline to seeing God. It is our job to keep working on the subconscious mind so that we can see and hear God clearly.

BLESSED ARE THE PEACEMAKERS

> *Blessed are the peacemakers, for they shall be called sons of God* (Matthew 5:9).

I thought of peacemakers as brilliant people who could get others in power to agree peacefully. That certainly wasn't me, so whoever these great minds were, I understood why they were super-blessed. There can't be anything more frustrating than trying to get two opposing sides to see eye-to-eye in a peace-ful way, especially if both sides are fighting against you. But look at the peace-makers in history. Many of them, like King David, were not peaceful in the moment, but their actions in the long run promoted peace. Being peaceful and being a peacemaker can be two entirely different things.

> **Being peaceful and being a peacemaker can be two entirely different things.**

BLESSED ARE THOSE WHO ARE PERSECUTED

Blessed are those who are persecuted for righteousness' sake, for theirs is the kingdom of heaven. Blessed are you when they revile and persecute you, and say all kinds of evil against you falsely for My sake. Rejoice and be exceedingly glad, for great is your reward in heaven (Matthew 5:10-12).

This irritated me because what value is there in being persecuted? My thought was, *If you persecute me, I am going to terrorize you.* So Jesus was one more time telling me to do the opposite of what I would naturally do. In fact, He says, "Rejoice and be glad, because great is your reward in Heaven." This is insane! You're telling me that I ought to be happy and actually rejoice when people do these awful things to me?

If I stood up for what was right and was persecuted and reviled as a result, it would be worth it because I would get the Kingdom of Heaven. And by the way, what was the Kingdom of Heaven? Could Jesus make it any more confusing? One moment He compares it to a certain king who wanted to settle accounts (see Matt. 18:23), then He compares it to a landowner trying to hire laborers (see Matt. 20), and then to a mustard seed (see Matt. 13:31), and then like leaven (see Matt. 13:33). And is the Kingdom of Heaven the same as the Kingdom of God? If so, then that triggers a whole other set of comparisons.

I certainly have experienced being persecuted and still have that experience to this day. Recently, I did the weekly Pentagon prayer breakfast in Washington, DC. One day it was attended by all generals and admirals. Afterward one general "Googled" me on the Internet and found some "dirt." He then complained to the head of the Christian embassy, and my image was tarnished. The general did not seem to realize that anyone can put something on the Internet; it doesn't mean that it's true. It hurts to be persecuted, especially when it seems unfair (make your own determination on the righteous part).

What I have learned is that until you can handle persecution the same as you handle success, you will never succeed. This Scripture is about adjusting your perspective. Handling people saying negative things about you is a way of building muscle. The muscle is necessary because *nothing great becomes great without overcoming great resistance.* If you want a great marriage or a great business or a great spiritual life, then you must be prepared for great resistance.

> **...nothing great becomes great without overcoming great resistance.**

This Scripture is telling us to not only endure persecution, but welcome it. I don't enjoy being persecuted. I don't think anyone does. But with this piece of Scripture in mind, I see that this is the very thing I need in order to get to my goal. I may not be "rejoicing," but I can get to an attitude of basically looking at the devil and saying, "That's the best shot you got?!" There is a certain satisfaction in that.

Don't get happy if everybody has only good things to say about you. Someone once said, *If you are running and the devil isn't chasing you, it's probably because you're running on the same team.*

> *If you are running and the devil isn't chasing you, it's probably because you're running on the same team.*

A Short Recap

- Being meek doesn't mean that you allow people to take advantage of you, but rather that you are submitted to God.

- When you are open to God, you will be blessed.

- Humility is key to entering the Kingdom of God.

- The pursuit of a pure heart is the thing that keeps you on the right path.

- Peacemakers are going to be super-blessed!

- Until you can handle persecution the same as you handle success, you will never succeed.

- After you have endured persecution, you may come out of it much stronger, wiser, and richer.

A Final Thought

Persecution is a reality of life. How you deal with it determines your greater outcome and reward. The best thing is to place it on the same level as the good things that come your way. Then you will not be forced to become haughty and prideful. I thought that this poem by Rudyard Kipling entitled "If" would be most appropriate to leave you with. The amazing thing about this wonderful poem is that the author suggests that we treat both success and failure as the same. It offers a balance to life, which is, I believe, a major point of the beatitudes.

If

If you can keep your head when all about you
Are losing theirs and blaming it on you,
If you can trust yourself when all men doubt you
But make allowance for their doubting too,
If you can wait and not be tired by waiting,
Or being lied about, don't deal in lies,
Or being hated, don't give way to hating,
And yet don't look too good, nor talk too wise:

If you can dream—and not make dreams your master,
If you can think—and not make thoughts your aim;
If you can meet with Triumph and Disaster
And treat those two impostors just the same;
If you can bear to hear the truth you've spoken
Twisted by knaves to make a trap for fools,
Or watch the things you gave your life to, broken,
And stoop and build 'em up with worn-out tools:

If you can make one heap of all your winnings
And risk it all on one turn of pitch-and-toss,
And lose, and start again at your beginnings
And never breathe a word about your loss;

If you can force your heart and nerve and sinew
To serve your turn long after they are gone,
And so hold on when there is nothing in you
Except the Will which says to them: "Hold on!"

If you can talk with crowds and keep your virtue,
Or walk with kings—nor lose the common touch,
If neither foes nor loving friends can hurt you;
If all men count with you, but none too much,
If you can fill the unforgiving minute
With sixty seconds' worth of distance run,
Yours is the Earth and everything that's in it,
And—which is more—you'll be a Man, my son!
—Rudyard Kipling[2]

POINTS TO PONDER

1. Which of the beatitudes listed in Matthew 5:3-12 do you find most challenging personally? Why? Which ones seem to come more easily? Why?

_____

_____

_____

2. "Once we think we know everything, there is no space for God or new knowledge." Have you ever fallen into this trap?

_____

_____

_____

3. "Being peaceful and being a peacemaker can be two entirely different things." Can you think of examples, either from the Bible or from your own life, of peacemakers who were not necessarily peaceful or of peaceful people who were not necessarily peacemakers? Do either of those describe you? Are you peaceful? Are you a peacemaker?

_____

_____

_____

4. "Nothing great becomes great without overcoming great resistance." What does that mean? Try rewriting it in your own words and ask yourself how it applies in your life.

_____

_____

_____

5. Search the Word of God for some Scriptures to help you through those times of great resistance and that help you understand your God-given purpose. Write them down. Memorize them if possible. Here are some examples to get you started: *"Be not overcome with evil, but overcome evil with good"*; *"For I know the plans I have for you, says the Lord. Plans to prosper you and not to harm you. Plans to give you a hope and a future"*; *"For we are more than conquerers...."*

_____

_____

_____

ENDNOTES

1. *Merriam Webster's New World Dictionary,* 2010, s.v. "submissive," http://www.merriam-webster.com/dictionary/submissive (accessed June 4, 2010).

2. Rudyard Kipling "If" 1899, Archive of Classic Poems, http://www.everypoet.com/archive/poetry/Rudyard_Kipling/kipling_if.htm.

OTHER BOOKS BY BRIAN KLEMMER

Five Great Sermons
(each sermon provided in both audio CD and in DVD)

Compassionate Samurai
Being Extraordinary in an Ordinary World

Eating the Elephant One Bite at a Time
52 Leadership Lessons

If How-To's Were Enough, We Would All Be Skinny,
Rich, and Happy

When Good Intentions Run Smack Into Reality
10 Ways to Get Unstuck

Available at www.klemmer.com/product or amazon.com
or call 800-577-5447

Go to www.klemmer.com and sign up for a FREE weekly leadership principle along with a story that illustrates the principle and two action items for the week. It's one thing to change. It's another thing to keep change changed. Also for FREE watch the champions online workshop and learn how to use James 2:17 to solve a problem when you have no idea what to do. It's an eye-opening revelation you can use to lose weight, make a marriage better, earn more money for a missions trip, or get a better job.

REFLECTIONS

_____

_____

_____

_____

_____

_____

_____

_____

_____

_____

REFLECTIONS

_____

_____

_____

_____

_____

_____

_____

_____

_____

_____

_____

REFLECTIONS

_____

_____

_____

_____

_____

_____

_____

_____

_____

_____

_____

_____

_____

REFLECTIONS

_____

_____

_____

_____

_____

_____

_____

_____

_____

_____

_____

REFLECTIONS

_____

_____

_____

_____

_____

_____

_____

_____

_____

_____

_____

_____

REFLECTIONS

_____

_____

_____

_____

_____

_____

_____

_____

_____

_____

_____

_____

REFLECTIONS

_____

_____

_____

_____

_____

_____

_____

_____

_____

_____

_____

REFLECTIONS

_____

_____

_____

_____

_____

_____

_____

_____

_____

_____

_____

_____

REFLECTIONS

_____

_____

_____

_____

_____

_____

_____

_____

_____

_____

_____

In the right hands This Book will Change Lives!

Most of the people that need this message will not be looking for this book. To change their life you need to put a copy of this book in their hands.

> *But others (seeds) fell into good ground, and brought forth fruit, some a hundred-fold, some sixty-fold, some thirty-fold* (Matthew 13:3-8).

Our ministry is constantly seeking methods to find the good ground, the people that need this anointed message to change their life. Will you help us reach these people?

> *Remember this—a farmer who plants only a few seeds will get a small crop. But the one who plants generously will get a generous crop* (2 Corinthians 9:6).

EXTEND THIS MINISTRY BY SOWING
3-BOOKS, 5-BOOKS, 10-BOOKS, OR MORE TODAY,
AND BECOME A LIFE CHANGER!

Thank you,

Don Nori Sr., Publisher
Destiny Image
Since 1982

18284560R00100

Made in the USA
San Bernardino, CA
28 December 2018